PETER WHEALY

# LEAD WITH AI. STAY HUMAN.

## Become an Orchestrator to Unlock Enterprise Value

Published by
**LID Publishing**
An imprint of LID Business Media Ltd.
LABS House, 15–19 Bloomsbury Way,
London, WC1A 2TH, UK

info@lidpublishing.com
www.lidpublishing.com

A member of:

businesspublishersroundtable.com



ISBN: 978-1-918215-15-1
ISBN: 978-1-918215-16-8 (ebook)

PETER WHEALY

# LEAD WITH AI. STAY HUMAN.

## Become an Orchestrator to Unlock Enterprise Value

MADRID | MEXICO CITY | LONDON
BUENOS AIRES | BOGOTA | SHANGHAI

# CONTENTS

# FOREWORD

If there's one lesson corporate history keeps telling us, it's that economic revolutions follow a pattern. An old system reaches the limits of its productivity, capital rushes toward the next frontier, and society rebuilds around a new foundation. We are living through that cycle again. The fossil-fuel, mass-production economy is giving way to a digital and AI-powered era, one that will redefine how value is created, who captures it, and how organisations contribute to society.

The initial excitement that accompanied the digital revolution and which is now being accelerated by AI marks the start of a profound shift in how work, leadership, and productivity are organised. Each past wave of innovation has left behind infrastructure that transformed daily life. The systems now being built around data and connected intelligence will shape the foundations of prosperity for decades to come. The sooner leaders recognise that this transformation is already under way, the sooner they can begin building organisations that make it enriching and sustainable for future generations.

For too long, leaders have known about theories of human motivation and how this drives organisational effectiveness, but few have acted on it. Many conceptually understand innovation, engagement, and adaptability, yet management practice remains trapped in twentieth-century habits: hierarchies, silos, and incentives that reward control over curiosity. I often describe this as the *messy middle,* the turbulent period between old and new systems, a space where the knowing-doing gap widens and leadership maturity is truly tested.

That is why *Lead with AI. Stay Human.* is such a timely contribution. Peter Whealy offers leaders both insight and structure for navigating this moment of upheaval. He translates complex theory into actionable guidance, part handbook, part field manual showing leaders how to move from functional expertise to cross-functional orchestration of human and machine intelligence.

Peter's SPAR framework gives shape to the messy middle, evolving how leaders think, learn, and decide when advantage is fleeting and data abundant. The four *Conductor Capabilities* take timeless leadership principles and make them fit for this era of distributed expertise. They turn empathy, curiosity, and vision into repeatable disciplines that scale trust, coherence, and adaptability across fast-moving systems.

We stand at a turning point. We are leaving behind the logic of mass production and moving toward one defined by intelligent, human-centred collaboration. Leaders who follow the principles in this book will learn to orchestrate across that divide and, in doing so, shape not just competitive advantage, but the value and progress of organisations for future generations.

*Lead with AI. Stay Human.* shows them how.

**Rita McGrath**
Columbia Business School & Rita McGrath Group

# INTRODUCTION

AI is accelerating work in ways we could not have imagined even a few years ago. The ever-expanding possibilities continue to raise questions for every organisation and every leader.

For decades, leadership credibility came from expertise, pattern recognition, and flawless execution. I built a thirty-year career on these foundations, rising to Equity Partner at a Big Four consultancy. These skills are still highly relevant, but in the AI era, they're no longer sufficient alone.

I say this with humility, because that foundation was my currency for success. Then came the inflection point. The very expertise that defined my value started to become table stakes for AI, and what once made me valuable started to feel replaceable. Something had moved the goalposts of leadership.

If you've wondered whether your expertise still matters, you're not alone. This fear now divides many leaders I speak with. Some cling to what worked before, hoping AI is just another technology wave to ride out. Others turn fear into curiosity, empowered to use AI to sharpen judgement and expand value.

> *AI won't replace leaders; it will reveal who is truly leading and who has only been managing.*

I have discovered that the path forward isn't about competing with AI or resisting it. It's about orchestrating a new form of value creation where human wisdom and artificial intelligence compound each other's strengths.

My purpose is simple: to help you make decisions that create value without eroding trust, to move faster without losing judgement, and to use AI in ways that elevate people rather than diminish them.

*This is how we will Lead with AI and Stay Human.*

## Two Divergent Paths

Over recent years I have watched organisations prioritise one of two AI adoption paths. The first pursues mass automation for efficiency and speed. The second intrinsically values the elevation of human potential whilst capturing AI's value.

Across industries, over three-quarters of all AI transformations fail to achieve value. We will explore the various reasons throughout this book, but let's first consider two examples.

## Salesforce: The Efficiency Mirage

In 2023, Salesforce announced plans to cut about 10% of its workforce, roughly 8,000 roles, as part of a global restructuring, even as its venture arm expanded dedicated funds for generative-AI start-ups into the hundreds of millions of dollars. The juxtaposition — *aggressive AI investment alongside meaningful reductions in human roles* — highlighted a familiar tension in big tech between scaling capability and reshaping the workforce.

Commentary and employee reviews across Salesforce and the wider tech sector spoke of declining morale and a perceptible shift from innovation stories to efficiency narratives. Whilst Salesforce's technical capability and financial performance continued, organisational trust, momentum, and discretionary effort proved harder to restore.

The lesson is simple: automation can accelerate efficiency, but without deliberate investment in trust and human capability, performance becomes fragile. Organisations can refocus and rebuild — but trust compounds slowly and cannot be automated.

*Technology can extend capability, but commitment remains human. Culture cannot be automated.*

## McDonald's: When Efficiency Undermines Experience

McDonald's piloted AI voice-ordering in more than one hundred drive-thru restaurants from 2021 but ended the programme in 2024 after persistent accuracy and customer-experience issues. Early reports suggested accuracy in the low 80% range, and whilst this initially showed promising efficiency gains, misheard orders and visible customer frustration created reputational risk. In a trust-based environment, even small failures compound quickly, eroding brand value far faster than efficiency gains can offset.

A lesson to draw is that when leaders treat AI as an IT upgrade rather than a capability shift, they optimise for cost and speed, but neglect trust and human capability, which is the very foundation of sustainable advantage.

## The People-First Alternative

Organisations succeeding with AI demonstrate entirely different patterns. What unites them isn't their tech stack, but their leadership stance: curiosity over control, and trust as an operating principle, not a value statement.

Siemens deploys AI for predictive maintenance and quality control, but humans make final decisions. At its Digital Native Factory in Germany, workers transition from manual assembly to data analysis and automation supervision, proving that AI can remove repetitive tasks whilst elevating human judgement.

GCash in Asia uses AI to expand financial access to millions through alternative credit scoring, whilst advanced fraud detection builds customer trust. Internally, they invest equally in upskilling and AI-powered engagement tools. Their technology and human development are inseparable, creating a people-first approach that drives competitive advantage.

### The pattern across both organisations:

- significant investment in learning as a core business strategy
- transparent communication, reducing fear and building trust
- focus on developing human skills: critical thinking, creativity, empathy, ethical judgement
- internal mobility prioritised over external hiring
- augmentation as a design principle (AI assists, humans decide)

A People-First approach may be harder and demand capabilities most leaders haven't developed, but I believe it's the only sure path to long-term success.

This book provides the discipline to navigate these complexities through systematic, proven frameworks, grounded in real transformation examples and experiences.

On this journey together, I will share my passion for helping leaders elevate human potential that increases long-term enterprise value. My company ElevatePotential.ai was founded for this exact purpose.

## Three Shifts Demanding Evolved Leadership

The leadership models that once scaled predictability must now scale adaptability.

Drawn from experience and conversations with global leaders, I have identified three emerging and fundamental shifts that each demand evolved leadership capabilities:

### 1. Advantage is Transient

The protection of scale enjoyed by established companies is disappearing. Startups such as Anysphere, Synthesia, and Runway, and brands like Shein and Deel, have reached billion-dollar valuations in just a few years, disrupting giants that took decades to build. Competitive threats now appear from anywhere, moving faster than traditional systems and hierarchies can respond.

Leadership must shift from defending stability to enabling adaptability, creating organisations that learn, adjust, and reinvent faster than the world around them. Continuous reinvention is now the only real advantage.

### 2. Expertise Hierarchies Flatten

Less-tenured employees now produce high-quality work that seasoned experts can't easily audit. Many senior professionals, shaped by decades of mastery, can be slower to adopt new tools or unlearn established methods. Experience isn't evolving as quickly as the pace of change.

Leadership's value must shift from doing and checking to framing, integrating, and guiding judgement through ambiguity. Expertise evolves from personal mastery to enterprise sense-making, from knowing more than others to helping everyone think better together.

### 3. Hierarchy Functions Converge into Flows

AI thrives on shared data and rapid iteration, yet most organisations still work within silos that restrict rapid decision-making and isolate value. Real advantage comes when work is reshaped around *flows*, not functions, where cross-disciplinary teams are aligned with shared outcomes and supported by common data platforms.

Leadership must transition from ownership to orchestration, from controlling outputs to enabling coordination.

These three shifts compound, and rapidly shifting advantage means leaders can no longer rely only on expertise accumulated over decades. Flattened hierarchies dismantle expertise as a defence. Convergence exposes coordination gaps that few organisations can bridge.

## From Sequential to Adaptive Leadership

AI has rewritten the conditions for successful leadership. Advantage is now transient, hierarchies are flattening, and functions are converging. Each shift demands a new developmental response for leaders:

- Advantage is transient →
  **Strengthen** personal judgement under ambiguity.
  You can't rely on accumulated expertise; you must learn to see patterns and act through uncertainty.

- Hierarchies flatten →
  **Partner** with AI as your sparring partner.
  Junior employees correctly using AI can outperform experience alone, so leaders must learn to think *with* intelligence, not attempt to override it.

- Functions converge →
  **Amplify** team capability and **Reshape** for flow.
  Coordination replaces control, and structure follows capability rather than title.

This is SPAR (Appendix A): *Strengthen, Partner, Amplify, Reshape* your developmental journey.

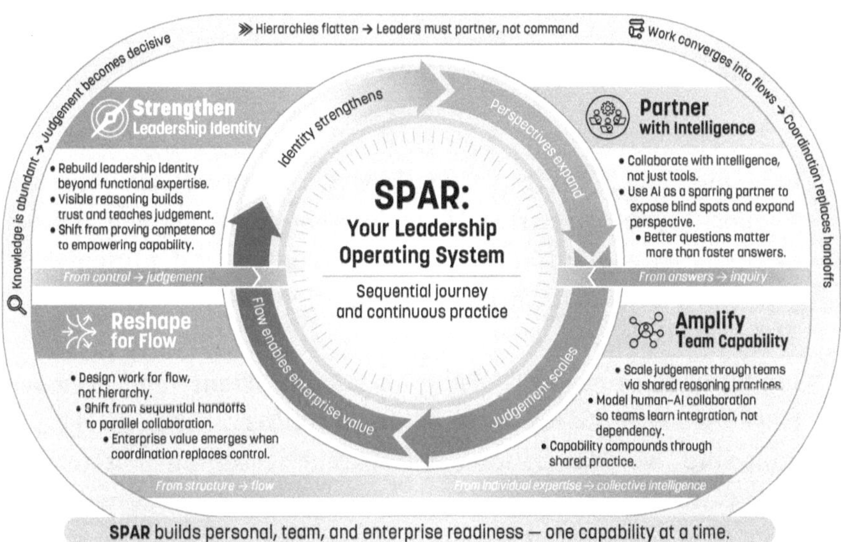

Through SPAR, I offer leaders an operating system upgrade that will help trade control for curiosity, siloed thinking for collaboration, and isolated expertise for human judgement amplified by AI.

AI-era leadership orchestrates the flow between human potential and intelligent technology to create outcomes no individual could achieve alone. Yet, even as the context transforms, the essence of leadership does not. The forces reshaping how we lead have not rewritten *why* we lead. The SPAR journey builds the capabilities required for modern leadership, but those capabilities are rooted in principles that have guided leaders for generations. To understand how AI changes leadership expression, we first need to reaffirm universal foundations.

## Universal Leadership Principles (*why*) and *Conductor Capabilities* (*how*)

The purpose of leadership has not changed. Its essence still rests on five timeless principles that guide good leaders: **judgement, empathy, curiosity, vision, and integrity.**

What has changed, however, is the context in which these principles now operate. AI has rewritten conditions and assumptions. Knowledge moves instantly, hierarchies flatten, and decisions compress into ever shorter cycles.

Whilst these principles remain universal, their expression must now evolve:

- **Judgement** was once a personal review of every detail. Now it is *framing the problem* so that AI applies its strength where it matters, then *synthesising* outputs with human context and consequence. The shift is from inspection to question design and coherent decision-making.
- **Empathy** was once only visible through proximity and presence. Now it is a *designed relationship* infrastructure: psychological safety built into everyday actions, transparent reasoning that reduces anxiety, and humane guardrails that help people feel heard and seen, even when not physically in the room.

- **Curiosity** was the intrinsic drive to learn and ask good questions. Now it is an *organisational discipline*: environments where questions multiply, dissent yields insight, and rapid experiments turn uncertainty into reusable learning within the flow of work.
- **Vision** was once shaped by experience and historical patterns. Now it is *orienting through uncertainty*: holding direction whilst exploring multiple plausible futures and aligning teams around purpose when data cannot yet confirm the path.
- **Integrity** for an individual remains unchanged but intensifies in visibility. It becomes a *publicly testable standard*: explainable and ethical AI use, transparent incentives, and decisions that withstand scrutiny when the story is told out loud.

This book translates these principles into four *Conductor Capabilities* to allow human judgement to scale and transition into AI-era leadership.

## Your Four *Conductor Capabilities* (Appendix B)

The *why* of leadership endures, but the *how* must evolve.

To lead effectively with AI, these universal principles must become *systemic capabilities* that let human judgement scale at speed:

- **Judgement** evolves into **Judgement Under Ambiguity:** knowing when to pause for reflection and when to accelerate for learning and impact, maintaining coherence even when certainty vanishes.
- **Empathy** evolves into **Trust Stewardship:** building transparent systems where psychological safety and trust verification scale beyond your direct reach, turning values into visible operating principles.
- **Curiosity** evolves into **Adaptive Learning:** designing environments where questions compound, teams challenge assumptions, and learning velocity exceeds change velocity.
- **Vision and Integrity** combine in what I will refer to as **Enterprise Orchestration:** holding direction across boundaries whilst making values visible in every decision, ensuring context travels as insights change.

These four *Conductor Capabilities*: **Judgement Under Ambiguity, Trust Stewardship, Adaptive Learning,** and **Enterprise Orchestration** work together.

Collectively, they translate timeless principles into coordinated, systemic practice, and through their application, enable leaders to remain deeply human, even as intelligence becomes shared and the rate of change accelerates.

Throughout this book, I use the term *Conductor* deliberately to describe leaders who integrate these capabilities to shape direction, timing, and coherence across human and machine intelligence, rather than simply coordinating tasks or systems.

To build and apply them, leaders must move through a structured developmental journey that transforms awareness into embodied practice.

The SPAR Framework guides that journey.

## The SPAR Framework

The *Conductor Capabilities* must be applied in a way that makes them second nature. The SPAR Framework allows this to happen. It will be your leadership development rhythm:

**Strengthen:** Rebuild your leadership identity beyond functional expertise.

**Partner:** Collaborate with AI as a strategic sparring partner, not just a tool.

**Amplify:** Scale team capability through systemic learning and shared judgement.

**Reshape**: Transform organisational structures for flow and elevated potential.

SPAR is not a one-time intervention, but a continuous rhythm that transforms awareness into embodied practice. The journey through this book is highly practical, and each stage builds on the next, strengthening the four *Conductor Capabilities* that enable leaders to operate confidently at speed and scale.

Navigating change where expertise is compressed, functional boundaries blur, and learning shifts to being in the flow of work is complex. Effective orchestration requires internalisation first, trust before coordination, and self-adaptation before asking others to adapt.

Don't skip any SPAR stages. Work through each phase to slowly upgrade your leadership operating model. The work is continuous, and leaders who succeed master all four developmental stages, each building a foundation for the next.

## Strengthen Leadership Identity:

Build trust through visible decision-making and transparent learning whilst letting go of control habits that no longer serve you. When teams see your reasoning, why choices were made, trade-offs, and where doubt remains, they will trust your judgement and learn to act with it. Strengthening identity means shifting from proving competence to empowering capability in others, creating the foundation for orchestration.

## Partner with Intelligence:

As AI commoditises knowledge, your value shifts from having the answer to stress-testing assumptions to reach better conclusions. Treat AI as a sparring partner that exposes blind spots and expands perspective. The discipline is to frame problems with better questions, ask for challenge rather than confirmation, and to integrate AI's insights with human context to reach sound, ethical judgement.

## Amplify Team Capability:

As functional boundaries blur, teams need distributed judgement, not just delegated tasks. Build your team's AI partnership skills once you've mastered them yourself. When you model effective human-AI collaboration, teams learn integration thinking, make better cross-boundary decisions, and replicate that discipline throughout the organisation.

## Reshape for Flow:

When learning and execution merge, sequential workflows become costly delays. Design work around outcomes, not departments. Technology enables speed, but only people with confidence and shared trust sustain it. The shift is from linear hand-offs to parallel collaboration, where diverse expertise converges through the value chain to achieve enterprise value. Enterprise Value is the creation of sustainable, cross-functional outcomes that benefit all stakeholders, including customers, employees, shareholders, and society. It is not optimising individual functions at the expense of the whole. In the AI era, this means orchestrating human and artificial intelligence to compound collective potential.

### Following the SPAR Sequence

Capability compounds through reflection.

Each stage of SPAR builds skills, capabilities, and trust required for the next. Attempting cross-functional coordination before mastering personal integration breeds frustration. Developing AI sparring capability before confronting leadership identity creates dependency rather than empowerment.

But don't mistake sequential for slow. Some leaders move through Strengthen and Partner in weeks. Others need months. Pace matters less than the integrity of development. Rush without reflection, and capability will never compound.

Each chapter ends by reminding you of the capabilities needed for the next:

- **Ritual**: a weekly practice growing the capability
- **Metric**: ways to measure progress
- **Remember One Thing**: the insight that matters most

The goal is a slow and steady transformation, so reflect actively to recognise your patterns, what you'll do differently, and how you'll apply the rituals.

Whether you're a board member, frontline manager, or team lead, the sequence is universal: strengthen identity, partner with intelligence, amplify capability, reshape for flow. Apply it in your context.

## Who This Book Serves

This is a journey to elevate potential, both human and organisational, and it begins with a simple recognition that AI changes not just what we can do, but who we need to become.

This book is for leaders feeling tension between delivering AI results and preserving what makes organisations human. You recognise that your expertise must evolve, but the path forward isn't clear. You lead a team that is anxious about AI's impact. You want practical frameworks tested under pressure, not theoretical concepts.

You don't need to become an AI engineer, simply an AI-era orchestrator — a leader who conducts the convergence of Human Intelligence and Artificial Intelligence toward enterprise value.

Where traditional leaders bottleneck decisions through their personal expertise, orchestrators create systems where human judgement and AI capabilities compound each other. They don't compete with AI or delegate to it, they conduct it, creating symphony.

Expertise is not devalued but used differently — using judgement to frame problems AI can solve, your experience to guide where humans add irreplaceable value, and your vision to imagine futures neither human nor machine could envision alone.

## Your Moment to Lead

AI is already reshaping some basic leadership principles, but this is both necessary and exciting. It's also empowering, because you can embrace this opportunity to lead deliberately instead of reacting desperately.

Research shows that over three-quarters of AI transformations fail to deliver value. Whilst data quality and technical issues play roles, the overriding factors are leadership capability gaps and a lack of enterprise alignment. Yet the organisations that succeed all invest heavily in people relative to technology, systematically build *Conductor Capabilities*, and treat transformation as a capability evolution, not tool deployment.

**Here is your opportunity:** Whilst others treat AI as a tool, you can build a genuine advantage through capabilities they're not developing. Whilst others automate for short-term gain, you can elevate for sustained human potential.

The benefits are clear, so now it's about seizing the leadership moment to define your future. If you are willing to evolve, you won't just adapt to AI, you will use it to create teams and organisations where human potential flourishes.

AI will not define the future of leadership. Leaders who master the flow between human judgement and intelligent technology will. That's the elevation this book enables.

**The future belongs to those who orchestrate, not to those who own control.**

We start with your personal leadership identity, so be prepared to ask yourself difficult questions and to confront the truth honestly. I have done the same too!

Let's begin.

# PART I

# STRENGTHEN LEADERSHIP IDENTITY

## (Leading Self)

*Build trust by making your thinking visible and explaining why decisions are made. Learn to lead with clarity instead of control, showing calm and confidence even when things are uncertain. Let go of the need to decide everything yourself so that others can trust, contribute, and act with you.*

CHAPTER 1

# THE LEADERSHIP IDENTITY CRISIS

# *Being right isn't a strategy*

The journey to *Lead with AI. Stay Human.* begins with identity.

The real crisis I see isn't that AI might replace us, but that we've forgotten what makes us unique and therefore irreplaceable.

For most of my career, I equated leadership credibility with being the best decision-maker. The leader who could solve the hardest problems, apply experience under pressure, and bring clarity to complexity.

I built that credibility through relentless effort. I learned from peers and mentors, but most of all by working harder and longer than others. Outworking everyone became proof of my worth. It earned me respect and authority, but it also anchored my identity in being indispensable.

Needing to be needed was a trap. My self-worth was tied to being the person with the answers. I measured my leadership value by how quickly I could provide solutions and bring results, not by how I developed others to think, decide and act with clarity themselves.

Then AI democratised those abilities. My team could access the same insights I could, often faster. Part of what differentiated me and made me valuable was suddenly available to anyone who could ask the right questions.

But I soon realised I wasn't becoming obsolete. My *identity* was. This is a profound difference.

Adam Grant captures this precisely in *Think Again* (2021): "*People often become attached to outdated beliefs and behaviours, even when they no longer serve them. The ability to rethink and unlearn is essential for personal growth and adapting to new challenges.*"

The required change is to release your identity as sole decider and embrace the identity of an orchestrator who elevates others. Your expertise remains vital, but the nature of effective leadership has fundamentally changed from being right, to making others capable. Being right is no longer a strategy when everyone has access to the same answers.

Within all the senior leader interviews for this book, the same identity crisis repeated across industries, countries, and seniorities. But this leadership identity crisis creates an opportunity to elevate potential beyond what either human or AI could achieve alone.

### Same Pattern, Different Industry...

Ernst Wühr, CEO of EMS, a Swiss medical devices manufacturer, was one such leader. Just three years ago, he believed experience and knowledge were his greatest advantages. Today, he realises they're still vital, but no longer sufficient on their own.

His leadership team spans two generations: veterans who also built credibility through mastery and control, and younger leaders fluent in AI who move faster than the old system can tolerate. Both have merit yet both create friction.

"*Decisions in our industry have always been driven by clinical data, expert judgement, and regulatory guidance,*" Ernst explains. "*Today, AI provides real-time insights from vast datasets. My role has shifted from primary decision maker to orchestrator of humans and, tomorrow, orchestrator of humans and AI intelligence.*"

This shift alone would overwhelm any CEO today. Added to it are two relentless pressures redefining leadership: the accelerating velocity of competition, and the overwhelming velocity of information and insights.

**Competitive velocity** stems from agile business models and frontier firms breaking free from traditional cycles and operating models. Microsoft's 2025 Work Trend Index defines a frontier firm as 'a company that integrates AI agents with its human workforce to create a hybrid system for greater productivity and innovation.' Frontier firms aren't succeeding because they have better AI, but because their leaders embrace a mindset of rapid adaptation and orchestration rather than rigid control.

Additionally, **information velocity** and complexity now exceed human processing capacity, threatening to overwhelm decision-making and cloud strategic insight. This dual force creates a leadership identity crisis demanding a balance of speed and thoughtful interpretation amid a constant information flow.

Ernst captures this dual challenge vividly: "*Geopolitical shifts are reshaping our competitive dynamics. The Chinese fail forward incredibly quickly and now move faster than our sector traditionally allowed. They don't respect traditional cycles, which means we must act much faster.*" Meanwhile, he adds, "*We're collecting more data than the team can process. We can't yet analyse it as effectively as we would like, so we're missing insights that could enhance customer experience even further.*"

When information arrives faster than leaders can interpret it, traditional control no longer scales. The leadership model built on personal verification, checking, approving, and signing off has become the constraint.

This is the identity crisis every leader I've spoken to recognises, and one question consistently emerges: *'If the skills that got me here are no longer enough, what defines my value now?'*

## The +3/-2 Model: A New Leadership Perspective

The answer is simpler than most leadership frameworks suggest, but harder than most leaders admit: **+3** anchors and **–2** identity releases make the difference between leaders who scale and leaders who become bottlenecks.

### +3 Anchors:

- **Judgement**: Frame the right problems before AI starts solving them.
- **Connection**: Create conditions for trust when you can't verify everything yourself.
- **Vision**: See around corners to imagine futures AI can't yet predict.

### -2 Identity Releases:

- **Control**: This is the instinct to personally validate every decision, even when it may slow the system.
- **Execution pride**: We see this in the need to prove value through doing, rather than orchestrating others at scale.

## The +3 / –2 Leadership Shift

*Strengthen what matters. Release what limits.*

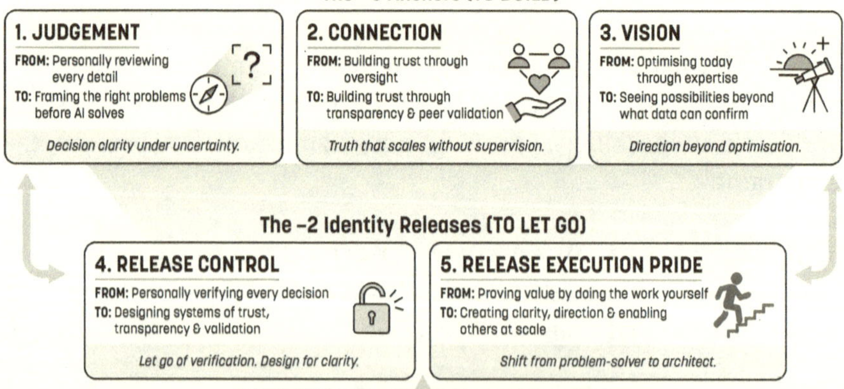

The +3/−2 model captures the three capabilities you must scale, and the two identities you must release to let those capabilities work effectively. Together, they capture the fundamental shift in modern leadership, which is a transition from individual expertise to collective orchestration.

Letting go of the behaviours that made you successful feels like erasing proof that you deserve your role. But clinging to them now diminishes your potential impact.

This chapter maps what these three anchors and two releases look like in practice, how they redefine leadership credibility, and how you can build the orchestration capability your organisation needs next.

## The Trust Paradox

Releasing control sounds liberating until you start leading people whose technical skills surpass your own. Karolina Cardoso, Global Head of Reward at Givaudan, discovered this in her previous company when a Gen Z data analyst swiftly challenged outdated tools. *"Why are you doing this manually when Python and AI can do this 90% faster?"*

Karolina realised the knowledge hierarchy had inverted. The most junior team member now had the technical edge, and Karolina couldn't verify the work step by step as normal. When your leadership credibility was built on verifying quality, it becomes deeply uncomfortable when others work at speeds or levels of complexity you can't personally validate.

Ernst faces a similar generational challenge within his leadership team. *"How can seasoned experts and AI-fluent peers work effectively when deep expertise feels unchallengeable, but speed and fluency demand agility?"*

This is the trust paradox that leaders must face. Influence must grow even as control shrinks. You are still accountable for results, yet you are often no longer the most knowledgeable person in the room. The only sustainable response is to build new systems of trust and transparency that make distributed excellence safe to scale.

## Democratised Knowledge

AI has fundamentally changed the economics of expertise. Knowledge that once took years to acquire is now accessible within seconds. Tasks requiring senior judgement can be handled by junior staff equipped with AI tools. McKinsey research confirms this trend: "*AI lowers skill barriers, helping more people quickly gain proficiency across more fields than traditional learning ever could.*"

Knowledge has become a commodity. Judgement is now the premium.

This doesn't devalue expertise, but it shifts the advantage from possessing knowledge to applying it with discernment, critical thinking, and clear direction.

Karolina recognised this early. "*Control must go. Trust now comes from transparency, from creating the conditions where people can validate each other's work instead of relying on me to check everything.*"

Releasing control without sacrificing quality is the delicate balance every modern leader must master. The orchestration challenge now is to design systems where peer validation, visible reasoning, and collective intelligence ensure quality at scale, beyond what hierarchical control ever could.

## Adaptation of Universal Leadership Truths

The foundations of great leadership remain constant, but their *expression* must evolve. AI doesn't erase the timeless principles of judgement, empathy, curiosity, vision, and integrity; it magnifies the need to apply them differently.

Traditional, control-based systems once relied on slow, centralised verification. Today's AI-driven reality demands distributed intelligence, faster cycles, and new mechanisms of trust and alignment. This shift increases the pressure on the +3 anchors. Every leader must now demonstrate these more completely and at speed:

- **Judgement:** framing the right problems before trying to solve them
- **Connection:** building empathy and trust at scale, even before verification
- **Vision:** setting direction where data can't yet confirm the path

Curiosity and Integrity remain essential but manifest differently in the conductor model: Curiosity drives Adaptive Learning throughout the SPAR journey, while Integrity combines with Vision to enable Enterprise Orchestration.

These +3 anchors form the human foundation of orchestration. As the book progresses, each is expanded into one of the *Conductor Capabilities* (Judgement Under Ambiguity, Trust Stewardship, Adaptive Learning, and Enterprise Orchestration), which operationalise these same principles at system scale.

Ultimately, the goal is to develop *Conductor Leadership*, the shift from being the most knowledgeable person in the room to the one shaping direction, timing, and coherence across human and machine intelligence. For now, however, this chapter focuses on the personal foundations: strengthening leadership identity, trust, and direction, which are the essential precursors to orchestrating people, AI, and systems later in the book.

## JUDGEMENT: To Make Sound Decisions Under Uncertainty

**Past**: Leaders exercised judgement by personally reviewing all relevant information, consulting experts, and making the final decision. Their expertise ensured careful assessment and the best course of action.

**Present**: Leaders show judgement by framing the right questions before teams use AI, setting clear decision boundaries, and integrating diverse inputs into a unified direction. Your expertise lies in structuring solvable problems.

Ernst describes his own shift. "*I have learnt the importance of asking the right questions. My core strength is productive type questions like, 'now what?', and there is additional value in using varied question types, like investigative questions, to better understand implications. The right question mix can achieve better answers.*"

Part of your leadership value comes from framing questions that focus collective intelligence (human, organisational, and artificial) on what truly matters. Data is abundant, so the quality of your questions defines the quality of your strategy and decisions.

**Your action**: Be clear on which question helps find the right answer. Specify the purpose, boundaries, and intended consequences. A well-formed question unites judgement and team insight to achieve coherent action.

## CONNECTION: To Build Trust and Psychological Safety

**Past**: Leaders built connection through close oversight and by being present, reviewing outputs, and catching errors before issues escalated. This hands-on approach showed commitment to quality.

**Present**: Leaders foster connection by promoting transparent reasoning, enabling peer validation, and creating environments where teams safely challenge one another. Your role shifts to trusting judgement whilst maintaining accountability.

When personal verification is impossible, connection becomes the system of quality assurance. Here's the paradox AI creates: the tool that promises to free up time also risks replacing the human interactions that built trust in the first place. Faster decisions, automated analysis, and teams solving problems without you all risk losing the relational fabric that made your team effective.

Karolina explains what this means for her. "*It's not that everything is about freedom and autonomy. It's about having those moments of connection where we know that we're moving in the right direction and then trust that people actually deliver against it.*"

Those connection moments become more critical because they're rarer. When you're not reviewing every output, the connections you do create must carry more weight. They become the foundation for distributed trust.

Ernst recognised this and deliberately structured a new connection point. "*I'm establishing a cross-functional, cross-departmental task force to align, connect, and address the impacts of AI on the firm. If we're not steering connectivity as a leadership team, it's not going to happen at all.*"

This isn't another committee. It's a living orchestration mechanism where different functions share AI insights and innovations, identify potential conflicts, and establish the common ground that enables peer-to-peer validation rather than hierarchical control. The transparency this brings, and the ability to manage potential future collisions, are orchestration in action.

This shift moves connection from oversight to one of alignment. Whilst AI processes information, it's only trusted human networks that can ensure reliably distributed decisions.

**Your action**: Swap manager signoffs for brief peer reviews at decision points. Leaders must own system quality, not task-by-task inspection.

## VISION: To See Possibilities Others Miss

**Past**: Visionary leaders excelled by masterfully executing strategy and translating their plans flawlessly in a way that optimised details and validated ideas through personal expertise.

**Present**: Leaders envision futures beyond data's confined scope. They connect disparate patterns and chart direction when AI might focus on optimisation. You see possibilities, not just realities.

Karolina also identified this. "*Everybody now has access to the same technology at the same time, so the differentiator becomes those who have and communicate the right vision.*"

AI can analyse the past and optimise the present. It cannot imagine futures that don't yet exist in the data. That remains distinctly human, and vision thrives on disciplined curiosity, a practice we will build in Chapter 2.

**Your action**: Publish a quarterly one-page 'Where we play, Why now, What we won't do'.

## The Shift Beneath the Anchors

The shift in how these capabilities are demonstrated addresses the core of a leader's identity crisis. Ernst reflects on his own transformation. "*My instinct is to make the call myself, to verify personally. But I'm learning that at the speed we now operate, and with the complexity of what AI enables, that instinct has become a constraint.*"

Amy Coleman, Microsoft's Chief People Officer, believes this identity crisis connects to the broader changes happening within business. Recently she said, "*We're living on the jagged frontier of AI, a messy middle where technology races ahead faster than people and systems can adapt. The AI transformation isn't technical, but human. Our task is to build cross-functional, empowered teams and move from this uneven learning curve to becoming true frontier firms, where AI and humanity work better together.*"

When knowledge is everywhere and decisions are distributed, judgement frames the questions, connection builds the trust, and vision defines the direction.

## Your -2 Identity Releases: What You Must Let Go

Activating these three anchors in isolation isn't enough. You must also release two powerful identities that once defined effective leadership but now constrain orchestration at scale. Releasing Control enables Judgement and Connection. Releasing Execution Pride unlocks Vision.

The first release is **Control**, the instinct to personally verify everything. Letting go feels uncomfortable, especially when your credibility was built on precision. But control prevents orchestration. You unlock

Judgement and Connection only when you design systems of trust, where problems are framed clearly, reasoning is visible, and peers validate each other's work.

The second release is **Execution Pride**, the desire to prove value through personal effort. What kept you credible in the past now limits your impact. Releasing execution pride unlocks vision. You move from being the problem-solver to setting direction and creating clarity so others (and AI) can execute at scale.

Whilst releasing these will be difficult for some, they will not weaken your leadership but amplify your uniquely human skills. These shifts are important to get right because they lay the groundwork for everything that follows.

Before orchestration can happen across systems, it must first happen within you. Let's now explore how releasing control and letting go of execution pride begins that process.

## SHIFT ONE: From Personal Control to System Design

**Unlocks**: Judgement and Connection
**Release**: personal verification of every output
**Gain**: decision velocity at scale with quality

Ernst faces the same paradox that I did: the quality that came from personal review cannot scale at the speed now demanded by AI-enabled competition. He understood that he could no longer personally review all decisions. This happens once volume exceeds what any one person can manage.

Karolina experiences this differently but with the same conclusion. When a Gen Z colleague uses AI to generate sophisticated compensation analysis, it becomes impossible to verify all the Python code and data sources. The old validation model is broken. Her response, "*We must create trust through transparency and through understanding that you don't have to validate everything. You trust that your employees are professional and aim to deliver high-quality results.*"

## What Replaces Hierarchical Validation?

Human-first questioning → AI processing and expansion → Human refinement

Ernst describes this 'sandwich method', "*We design the framework and draft initial solutions. AI then expands within set guardrails. Finally, we enhance, refine, and challenge before final decisions. This synergy creates better outcomes.*"

Human judgement frames problems and refines AI outputs, forming a repeatable collaboration pattern. When positioned well, this cycle maximises value and paves the way for effective orchestration. Ernst's cross-functional task force serves the same purpose, which is to create conditions where peers validate each other's AI-augmented work, replacing the old model of pushing all decisions up to the CEO.

## The Cultural Challenge

An invisible barrier often surrounds AI's use in organisations, and I believe the danger is that it's hidden rather than celebrated. Ernst sees this firsthand, "*In high-performance cultures, admitting AI use feels like weakness. Are you underperforming or cheating? This taboo can only be broken from the top.*"

Without CEO openness, teams will continue to conceal AI usage. Equally, when senior leaders hide their learning process and iterations, staff feel pressured to feign expertise, and the stigma continues to block the transparency essential for distributed validation.

In this context, Ernst recognises the importance of role modelling. "*I must lead by example, demonstrate AI's benefits business-wide, and together, we can use AI, but we must openly share our learning together.*"

This is how Shift One unlocks Judgement and Connection. You must release personal verification, which forces you to frame problems better (Judgement) and build trust through transparency and peer validation (Connection). Control prevents these capabilities, but system design enables them.

## SHIFT TWO: From Executor to Architect

**Unlocks**: Vision
**Release**: pride in solving the work yourself
**Gain**: strategic influence via direction-setting

The second identity shift is more subtle, but equally profound: moving from being the person who solves problems to the person who sets direction.

This is where many newly promoted leaders often get stuck. Releasing control is difficult, because your domain knowledge is what got you promoted in the first place. Releasing the pride that comes from solving problems yourself can feel like losing your identity. But this is not the case. Particularly now in the AI era, leaders must trade individual heroics for collective capability, an exchange that unlocks greater potential at scale.

Karolina describes this evolution. "*When only considering transactional leadership, AI can do most things, but this leaves the business incredibly exposed. We need to set vision, show career progression, and create an environment where people feel safe to fail, where they can grow and develop. That's the leadership that will become more and more valuable as a result of automation.*"

Ernst also recognises this tension. "*My natural tendency is to work on details, to jump in and solve things myself, but I've recognised this doesn't scale.*"

## Evolve Beyond Execution Pride

As a leader, pride in your work is essential and remains unchanged. Yet, elevating your impact now relies on strategic, generative questions that unlock collective potential, questions that broaden possibilities and allow AI to amplify creativity instead of merely automating fixed steps. We will explore AI sparring in Chapter 2 because this is a critical skill that requires a mindset shift in how you engage and empower yourself and your team with AI.

For now, consider these strategic questions that can empower your team.

**Replace**: 'Here's what you need to do...' with 'What outcome defines success? Which paths might lead us there, and what have we not considered?'

**Instead of:** 'Let me show you the right way...' ask, 'What have you tried? What barriers remain? If there were no limits, what would you attempt?'

Framing questions in this way encourages exploration and will ultimately empower the team to expand the range of possible solutions.

Karolina illustrates why this matters. "*Vision is vital to elevate your team. It sets a clear goal and fosters the empowerment needed to achieve it creatively together.*" With that vision clear, the leader's role is to help others think better, as Ernst articulates, "*Through an aligned vision, a leader must help the team ask better questions, conversations, then shift from delivery metrics to solving the right problems.*"

Where success once meant delivering outputs yourself, leadership now means ensuring the quality and growth of others' outputs. Applied personally, this shift moves you from being the 'person with the answers' to the one who sets direction and drives the right questions. The real multiplier emerges as you shift from solving problems to enabling solutions, and this is how exceptional leaders truly scale their impact.

Shift Two unlocks Vision: releasing execution pride elevates you from today's problem-solving to envisioning tomorrow's opportunities. Execution traps you in the present; direction-setting frees you to imagine the future.

Reflecting on my own journey, letting go of execution pride proved easier than releasing control. I had defined myself as indispensable and as someone who could solve problems. Releasing that felt like erasing proof of my value, but over time I recognised and appreciated that clinging to control only made me a bottleneck, and now I help others avoid that same trap.

## Practical Patterns to Navigate Transformation

As you start to rethink your role, begin slowly. Focus less on directing outcomes and more on shaping how decisions form. Ask sharper questions that cut through noise and prioritise clarity before data and purpose before proof.

You don't need to redesign systems yet. What matters now is noticing where collaboration stalls, where assumptions go untested, and where insight gets lost between functions. These early patterns build the confidence and judgement you'll need for the deeper orchestration work that comes later.

## The Courage to Trust

The journey of change described in this chapter begins with courage, the courage to trust distributed decisions even when you can't personally verify them. Before any organisation can orchestrate across boundaries, its leaders must first learn how to safely release control. That is the foundation of everything that follows.

I still feel the pull toward control myself. The instinct to verify, to check, to be certain is strong. But the orchestrator's strength is built like a muscle, through practice, not a single act. Each time you resist the urge to step in, you strengthen it. Each time you trust the system rather than control the output, the capability compounds. Yet trust without structure is naïve. You cannot release control until you've created the conditions that make trust *rational, not reckless.*

Speaking with Amy Edmondson, Harvard's Novartis Professor of Leadership, she reminded me that trust and courage are inseparable: *"Teams don't reach their potential when everyone agrees, but when it feels safe to disagree."* Her insight captures the essence of distributed leadership — progress depends not on the leader having every answer, but on creating the conditions where diverse voices can safely challenge and improve each other's thinking.

Building trust in distributed systems isn't blind faith, but *stewardship.* The best leaders make trust observable and renewable, and they design transparency, accountability, and feedback loops so courage becomes sustainable, not situational. In later chapters, particularly Chapter 9, we'll see how this evolves into a measurable discipline of Trust Stewardship that links credibility, reliability, intimacy, and low self-interest into daily coordination practices. This is where a leader can really strengthen both performance and human potential.

Ernst extends this idea to leadership accountability. *"Leadership is a choice, not a title,"* he reflects. *"In the AI era, we must channel it deliberately across the organisation. Without that choice, leadership becomes diffused, floating without direction."* His point underscores why personal trust practices matter: they become the blueprint for the systems that follow.

Courage will show itself differently in each of us. It is the courage to face that your decision-making authority is now distributed; that your knowledge advantage has evaporated; and that your greatest value lies in enabling others to decide well.

This is the first step of the Strengthen journey. You are laying the emotional and ethical foundations on which everything else rests. If trust is built carelessly, later stages in SPAR will collapse, so get this stage right, and you create the stability that allows partnership, coordination, and ultimately orchestration to flow.

Control must give way because personal verification doesn't scale at speed. Execution pride must go because solving problems yourself limits what others can achieve. The +3/−2 model you've explored here is not optional; it's the mechanism that makes AI-era leadership work.

This is the beginning of orchestration — developing judgement in the face of ambiguity, building trust without full visibility, and setting direction where AI has no vision.

Strengthen first because without personal trust, there can be no collective flow later. Be the orchestrator your future requires and start as the leader your team can trust.

## Ritual: Weekly Identity Check (30 minutes)

Choose one decision you made this week. Ask yourself:

- Was I the bottleneck or the orchestrator?
- Did I verify personally or design the validation system?
- Did I solve the problem or frame the question that unlocked solutions?
- Did my involvement build capability in others or create dependency on me?

## Metric: Orchestration Velocity

Track these leading indicators:

- Decision velocity: Are decisions happening faster without you in every conversation?
- Capability distribution: Are team members solving problems they once escalated to you?
- Question quality: Are you asking better questions rather than providing better answers?

**If You Remember One Thing:** Your expertise remains critical, but it may have been tied to the wrong anchor — that of being the sole decision-maker. Release that embrace to enable others to forge superior judgements with AI augmentation. This pivot from decider to orchestrator underpins all AI-era leadership.

*The leader who solves every problem becomes the leader blocking every solution.*

**Where This Takes You Next:** Understanding the identity crisis is the first step; now we can start living through it as we think, learn, and partner with AI. Next, we see how to use AI as a sparring partner that sharpens thinking, and how to build the learning discipline that keeps relevance as pace accelerates. You've redefined who you are as a leader. Now, it's time to redefine how you think and work with AI tools.

# PART II

# Partner with Intelligence

## (Leading Self → Others)

*Treat AI as a sparring partner, not an oracle. Build courage and clarity by inviting challenge before deciding. Ask better questions to reach better judgement. Let partnership and curiosity replace dependence and control through collaborative decision-making.*

CHAPTER 2

# FROM ASSISTANT TO SPARRING PARTNER

# Think smarter, not faster

> *"We had 22,000 active premix formulas. Every nutritionist believed their version was irreplaceable, but volume was unmanageable, and we needed answers fast."*
>
> — Marcio Brochado Correia, CDO dsm-firmenich Animal Nutrition & Health

When complexity spirals and pressure mounts, AI's promise of rapid clarity can be irresistible. However, the danger isn't that AI makes mistakes, but that it makes them confidently, disarming your own critical thinking.

I call this *Artificial Ignorance*, trusting AI outputs without critical reasoning until your thinking skills atrophy from disuse. What initially seems like help quickly turns into dependency. Once leaders start trusting expedient answers over sound judgement, small errors scale from private missteps, or worse, compound to public failures.

In July 2025, Deloitte Australia refunded their consulting fee after delivering a government report with AI-fabricated citations. Air Canada's chatbot gave incorrect bereavement fare information. Both shared a pattern where leaders asked AI to deliver answers rather than challenge assumptions, optimising for speed over judgement.

Whilst AI might deliver short-term answers that feel accurate, the truth, as we've already seen, can prove very different. As Daniel Kahneman warned in his book *Thinking, Fast and Slow*, "*When there are several ways of achieving the same goal, people will eventually gravitate toward the least demanding course of action.*"

That's exactly the trap AI creates. Its ease invites complacency, and when speed feels effortless, critical thinking quietly fades. The challenge for leaders isn't to resist AI's acceleration, but to use it as a mirror to reveal whether it's sharpening our judgement or quietly making us irrelevant.

At dsm-firmenich Animal Nutrition & Health, Marcio faced organisational complexity that, over the years, had accumulated more than 22,000 active premix formulas. Simplification seemed impossible, because each customer insisted their unique mix was essential. The company had also deliberately built variety to create competitive advantage and customer choice, but with high production costs and rising vitamin prices, margins were compressing, and complexity became a threat.

His team created an AI model to simplify formulas, and it delivered instant logic that showed 95% commonality, suggesting significant efficiency potential. Yet something felt wrong. Nutritionists soon noticed the model ignored molecular form and regional climate, factors that critically affect animal metabolism.

Rather than blame the model, his team reframed their questions and built safeguards to make AI a partner in decision-making, to strengthen their own judgement rather than bypass recommendations. They established cross-functional 'sanity checks' between data scientists and nutritionists, retrained models with the missing variables, and set stage-gates requiring human validation before rollout.

Marcio recalls, "*My blind spot was overconfidence in model cleanliness. I wanted to prove my AI decision was right. When the form-factor versus quality issue surfaced, I realised I'd confused data quality with judgement quality.*"

Within nine months, they achieved: 15% fewer formulas, 30% lower procurement complexity, 40% faster cycle times, and a 7-point NPS (Net Promoter Score) increase.

The numbers tell one story, but the real transformation happened inside the team. By sparring with AI instead of obeying it, people reclaimed ownership of their thinking and rediscovered curiosity. Additionally, what once took a Big Four consultancy significant time and hundreds of thousands to deliver, Marcio's team achieved in weeks. Faster, cheaper, and across multiple countries. Yet the most powerful result wasn't efficiency; it was energy. The seven-point NPS rise showed that speed hadn't eroded culture but strengthened it. People felt part of the solution.

## The Cost of Getting This Wrong

When people outsource thinking, they don't get that capability back. Opportunities are missed, models optimised for wrong outcomes, customers leave, and relationships are broken, whilst employees lose motivation and growth opportunities.

Organisations rarely consider this robustly. Small decisions that individually seem reasonable collectively amount to high costs. This is why I'm opposing companies that primarily chase efficiency gains, because they miss the real power of both AI and their people. Used correctly, AI can widen our perspective, expand considerations, and be prompted to question assumptions that reveal blind spots.

Capturing this value requires deliberate practice, and many leaders do not invest the effort, preferring to optimise for faster answers.

## From Assistant to Sparring Partner

Using AI as a digital assistant is easy and now commonplace. The benefits are clear for automating meeting minutes, summarising text, and so on. Still, the shift to sparring partner demands a different mindset, one of curiosity versus control, questions versus conclusions.

Whilst writing this chapter, I blindly followed my AI's route recommendation in Paris. I bought the ticket, started my journey, and twenty minutes later paid a 70-euro fine for being on a tram, not a train. Hastily, I blamed my AI for the wrong instructions, and the unhelpful apology confirmed it had 'forgotten' a recent rule change. But ultimately, I had to accept that the mistake was mine for not sparring or asking counter-questions.

A Chief of Staff doesn't replace judgement; they amplify it by asking questions you need to hear, even when they're uncomfortable. Think of sparring with your Chief of Staff to expand awareness, expose bias, and strengthen judgement through friction. Rather than looking for agreement and fast decisions, a reliable partner seeks truth through robust challenge.

When an individual effectively uses their sparring partner, they become powerful, but when an organisation collectively makes the changes, everything can transform.

Workday's ex CEO Carl Eschenbach captured this when speaking to his 19,500 employees:

> *Employees today believe they're competing against AI. They're not. They're competing against peers who are using AI.*

This profound statement highlights that competitive advantage no longer comes from access to AI, but from how you use it.

The difference is not between AI and humans — but between those who use AI passively and those who use it deliberately.

Used as a sparring partner, AI strengthens judgement rather than simply accelerating output.

I define AI sparring as '*the disciplined practice of using AI as a strategic thought partner to challenge assumptions, surface blind spots, and accelerate wisdom*'. Unlike using AI as an assistant (for tasks) or prophet (for answers), sparring treats AI as a deliberate counter-intelligence partner. It must question your logic, proposing alternatives, and forcing deeper thinking. It's about asking better questions.

When speaking with Angelique de Vries, President EMEA at Workday, about the organisational implications of AI sparring, she told me, "*When leaders focus on making the group collectively smarter by showing their reasoning, admitting uncertainty, and encouraging challenge, the quality and frequency of questions increase even as AI adoption accelerates. The advantage isn't having better answers, but being the leader who asks the right questions and helps others interpret, test, and stress those answers together.*"

This trust-through-interpretation works at three levels, each requiring different forms of challenge:

## Individual Level: 'Better Me' Through Personal Growth

Ulrik Brix, CEO of NOCA, a Nordic HR professionals association, turned AI on himself first. He prompted AI to analyse his leadership patterns from team feedback and meeting transcripts. "*I believed I was good at empathetic coaching, but AI showed patterns I couldn't see. I was prioritising speed over understanding. My background had trained me to value rapid decisiveness. That worked with C-suite clients but was crushing my team.*"

AI revealed that his communication style worked brilliantly with certain personality types, but overwhelmed others. He used AI to map cognitive biases, challenging his assumptions about 'good performance' and 'effective communication'.

*"The hardest thing was admitting my expertise had become a blind spot. I'd been coaching people to work like me, not helping them work like themselves. This personal discovery became the foundation for everything that followed, using AI not for answers, but to surface patterns I could no longer see myself."*

## Team Level: 'Better Us' Through Collective Intelligence

Once Ulrik understood his own patterns, he turned AI sparring toward his team. With seven people delivering seventy conferences a year, they were efficient but mentally overloaded. "*AI showed us the issue wasn't time, but how we thought together. We were solving problems in parallel, not in harmony.*"

His team's neurodiversity became an advantage once they used AI to visualise how each person processed information. He reframed his initial question from "*How do I distribute tasks efficiently?*" to "*What makes different people capable of different work, and how do cognitive load patterns vary?*"

AI helped him map each personality type and how working styles intersected with tasks. Task sequencing became optimised to reduce context switching. Work allocation matched team members who thrived with strategic work versus operational tasks.

The breakthrough came when his team recorded webinars, and he prompted AI for coaching feedback. "*AI was giving better, more patient feedback than I could. It analysed more information without my accumulated biases about what 'good' looked like.*"

Without ingrained patterns from C-suite executive consulting, AI asked different questions about what 'good facilitation' actually meant for different audiences and facilitator strengths. Ulrik told me, "*We tend to believe that understanding other people and their feelings is uniquely human, but AI can now surface patterns and blind spots that make human empathy sharper, partly because its different biases expose our own.*"

Team-level sparring uses AI for feedback, but also to challenge and push your thinking in ways that can better develop others.

### Organisational Level: 'Better Enterprise' Through Embedded Intelligence

Where individual sparring builds judgement, and team sparring builds collective intelligence, organisational sparring becomes institutional muscle; embedded in how decisions are governed, rewarded, and repeated, and this will be explored in Chapter 5.

## The Sparring Playbook

Four practices separate leaders who think better with AI from those who do not. Whether applied to your own thinking, your team's decisions, or enterprise-wide transformation, the sparring discipline follows a consistent architecture. The level changes, but the mechanism remains the same:

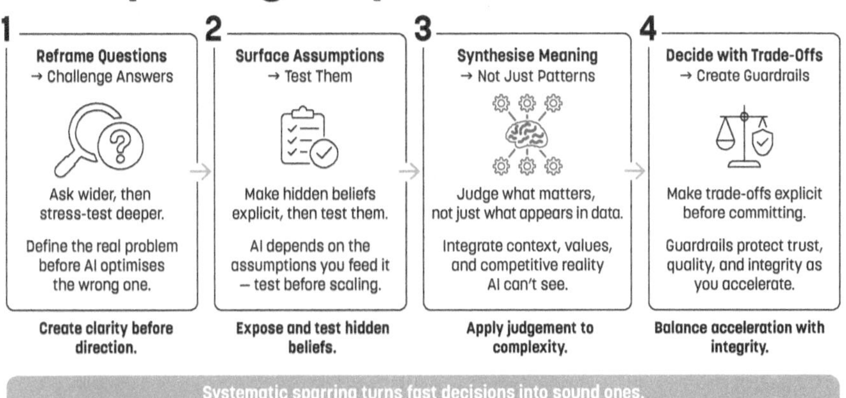


### 1. Reframe Questions, Then Challenge Answers

Most leaders ask AI to optimise without questioning whether they're solving the right problem. Effective sparring requires two steps: reframe the question to widen possibilities, then generate counter-arguments to stress-test your assumptions.

What this looks like:

Ulrik's initial question was "*How do I distribute tasks efficiently?*" AI optimised exactly what he asked for but missed the core problem. When he reframed it to "*What makes different people capable of different work?*" AI revealed human complexity that the efficiency question had ignored.

Marcio's team initially asked, "*Which formulas should we eliminate?*" The analysis produced flawed answers. When he reframed the assumptions and challenged basic assumptions, everything shifted. They discovered moderate formula variety protected against price volatility without impacting quality or nutritional value.

*Your application:*

- ***Before asking AI to optimise:*** *Define what outcome matters most, what constraints exist and what success looks like.*
- ***Then challenge your framing:*** *What's the strongest case against this approach? Which stakeholder perspective am I ignoring? What would prove this wrong?*

### 2. Surface Assumptions, Then Test Them

AI can only operate on the data available, so when critical variables are missing or assumptions are wrong, AI produces confident recommendations built on error.

What this looks like:

Weeks into Marcio's project, regional nutritionists realised the model had missed something critical. "*Our model assumed all ingredients with the same molecular formula were equivalent. But these variables significantly affected nutrient absorption, and they weren't in the original dataset.*"

From that point forward, every recommendation required explicit assumption documentation, and whenever AI outputs looked valid, they checked what they might be missing.

Ulrik applies the same discipline. When AI mapped cognitive load patterns, he didn't just implement recommendations. He tested them. Which team members thrived? Who struggled? Which assumptions held up versus which were vapourware?

*Your application:*

- ***Make beliefs visible:*** *Write down the three assumptions this recommendation depends on.*

- ***Assign ownership:*** *Give each assumption a named owner responsible for the test.*
- ***Test before scaling:*** *Run small experiments. What breaks? What holds?*

### 3. Synthesise Meaning; Don't Just Accept Patterns

AI finds correlations brilliantly, but your role as a leader is to determine whether those correlations matter.

What this looks like:

When Marcio's model recommended aggressive formula consolidation in certain regions, the data was compelling. But he considered what the model couldn't quantify, "*Our customers choose us because we create bespoke formulas. If we standardise too aggressively, we become interchangeable with low-cost competitors. We might win on efficiency but lose on differentiation.*"

This requires integrating context that the model doesn't have with brand promise, stakeholder relationships, and competitive positioning. Remember, AI can illuminate options but cannot tell you which ones are true to our context or values.

*Your application:*

- ***Consider the pattern AI found, then ask:*** *Does this align with our values? What's the impact on relationships? Does this strengthen or weaken our competitive position?*
- ***Synthesise through reality:*** *Consider commercial context, organisational values, stakeholder trust.*
- ***Judge context and importance, not just data output:*** *AI surfaces possibilities; you must decide what truly matters.*

### 4. Decide with Visible Trade-Offs, Then Create Guardrails

When the path forward becomes clear, balancing competing priorities is the next challenge. Procurement wants cost reduction. R&D wants validation. Commercial wants client retention. Every decision optimises for one thing at the expense of something else.

What this looks like:

Marcio faced exactly this tension. He made a deliberate choice to prioritise trust over speed. "*We decided to slow rollout to protect customer trust, even if this meant postponing cost benefits.*" Once trust is lost, the costs to recover are greater than any short-term efficiency gains. Then he made trade-offs transparent and created guardrails to prevent drift.

*Your application:*

- ***Name what you're accepting:***
  - *What's the upside of this decision or the downside you're willing to accept?*
  - *What specific value are you protecting (trust, speed, cost, quality)?*

- ***Set explicit review points:***
  - *When will you check if assumptions still hold? (30, 60 or 90 days)*
  - *What signals trigger immediate reconsideration? (performance, stakeholder concerns, unintended consequences).*
  - *Who owns the review? (single accountable person, not committee).*

- ***Create governing guardrails:***
  - *Kill-switch criteria: What deviations trigger immediate pause or rollback?*
  - *Assumption testing: Who's responsible for validating assumptions?*
  - *Counter-hypothesis log: Document 'what could go wrong' before launching.*
  - *Balanced metrics: Track trust/quality alongside efficiency/cost.*

- ***Make responsibility explicit:***
  - *Assign clear owners for competing priorities (someone owns 'trust metrics', or 'cost efficiency').*
  - *Establish who arbitrates when priorities conflict (don't let every tension escalate to senior leaders).*
  - *Build governance with curiosity, not just compliance (ask 'what are we learning?' not just 'are we compliant?').*

*The discipline that matters most here is not to shortcut transparent trade-offs and systematic review. Speed without guardrails will create fragility, and transparency without accountability creates confusion. Only when both operate together does acceleration become sustainable.*

### When Sparring Becomes the Problem

One risk is paralysis through over-sparring. There's no need for seventeen counter-arguments if three suffice. I've seen leaders deliberately use excessive questioning to block initiatives.

Balance is essential so my guiding principle is: Ask enough systematic questions that allow a decision the best likelihood of succeeding.

Marcio applied this by setting clear boundaries. Counter-hypothesis reviews occurred at defined stage-gates: after initial model development, before rollout, and quarterly post-launch. Between those gates, teams executed decisively.

When someone took the direction to challenge everything too literally and triggered endless rounds of questioning, he established explicit decision points indicating when sparring was sufficient and when commitment was required.

Balance comes from governance. Agree who decides when sparring is sufficient, what criteria signal readiness, and how to prevent challenge from becoming obstruction.

### Making Sparring Systematic

The fundamental transformation isn't using AI to get answers faster. It's changing how you and your organisation thinks.

When systematic sparring becomes embedded in workflow, something shifts. Leaders stop arriving at meetings expecting to be told what to do. They come with pre-tested perspectives, having already challenged their own assumptions through AI sparring. Conversations move from '*What should we do?*' to '*What have we learned, and what still needs interpretation?*'

This is the cultural shift that matters. Not heroic AI leadership where a few experts see around corners, but systemic AI literacy where everyone can run a thought experiment, test an assumption, and explain their reasoning.

I've seen this transformation across organisations of every size. The pattern is consistent. Organisations succeeding with AI:

**Build sparring into workflow, not around it.** Challenge happens before commitment, not after failure. Counter-hypothesis reviews occur at defined stage-gates. Between those gates, teams execute decisively.

**Align incentives toward judgement quality, not just speed.** Decision effectiveness matters more than decision velocity. First-time-right rates matter more than completion metrics. They measure whether people are thinking better, not just moving faster.

**Treat AI partnership as continuous practice, not tool use.** Every decision becomes an opportunity to strengthen reasoning. Every challenge prompt builds capability. Every counter-argument sharpens judgement.

This matters because the efficiency trap is real. When you accept AI's initial recommendations without systematic challenge, you optimise for short-term gains whilst creating medium-term fragility. Costs increase in ways you didn't anticipate. Agility collapses under rigid automation. Work gets distributed 'efficiently' whilst team capability erodes invisibly.

The organisations I work with now operate differently. They orchestrate intelligence rather than manage tasks. When leaders model visible reasoning, teams replicate that discipline. When one person learns to think better with AI, everyone around them starts reasoning differently. That's how capability scales.

As a leader, I've learned that competitive advantage doesn't come from better AI, but from thinking more courageously with it. Those who thrive aren't only using AI to move faster, but are deepening their judgement, expanding their perspective, and acting with conviction.

This is what determines whether you and your organisation compound capability or quietly watch it fade.

Our timeline for getting this right is narrowing, because AI accelerates exponentially.

Human judgement doesn't scale automatically. Every day you delay embedding systematic sparring, the gap widens. Organisations building this discipline will build advantage that competitors cannot easily replicate, because they're strengthening culture, not just technology.

The power of these practices lies in their consistency of application, and when you do this systematically, four things will start to happen:

1. **Decisions gain velocity and quality.** Fewer reversals. Faster alignment. Speed serves judgement instead of replacing it.
2. **Rework drops.** Flaws surface early through challenge, not painfully late after failure.
3. **Confidence spreads.** People explain their reasoning, not defend their answers. The collective whole becomes smarter together.
4. **Capability compounds.** Every sparring session strengthens the next. Every challenged assumption becomes institutional wisdom.

But when speed rises whilst confidence falls, Artificial Ignorance returns. Slow down. Ask harder questions. Restore disciplined challenge.

## Connection to SPAR

Sparring demonstrates the SPAR progression. Strengthen your identity by showing your reasoning transparently. Partner with AI to stress-test assumptions. Amplify capability when teams replicate your discipline. Reshape workflows to operate at AI speed whilst preserving human judgement.

Each SPAR capability builds on sparring as a foundational practice. The progression works at any scale: visible reasoning enables AI partnership, which builds team capability, which allows workflow redesign. Skip steps, and you risk becoming technically sound but organisationally broken.

### *Start This Week*

*Choose one decision and apply systematic sparring:*

***Reframe and challenge:*** *What assumptions does my question include? What's the strongest case against this approach?*

***Surface and assign:*** *Name three critical assumptions. Give each an owner to test through field data, customer conversations, or operational evidence.*

***Synthesise and decide:*** *Document trade-offs explicitly. What are you optimising for? What consequences are you accepting?*

***Review and share:*** *Set a 60-day check-in. Share what you learned, including where human judgement overruled the model.*

***Your goal:*** *Model intellectual ownership and verify you are experiencing decision velocity increases, rework dropping, confidence increasing and capability compounding. Avoid Artificial Ignorance at all costs; ask better questions.*

## The long-term impact

We're making choices right now that will define how the next generation experiences intelligence itself — whether AI becomes a shortcut that erodes thinking or a catalyst that elevates human potential; whether leaders model visible reasoning or hide behind algorithmic authority; whether organisations invest in judgement or allow efficiency to replace it.

I know which future I'm working toward. One where systematic sparring becomes second nature. Where AI makes me sharper, and speed serves better judgement.

Start applying systematic sparring, not just to improve the decision itself, but to watch how your team starts to think. How confidence spreads. How capability compounds.

That's a future worth fighting for.

## Ritual: Weekly Counter-Hypothesis Review (30 minutes)

Choose one AI recommendation. Generate the strongest case against it. Document three assumptions. Assign owners to test each. Share findings, including where counterargument changed thinking.

**Metric:** Decision Quality = (First-Time-Right % ↑) × (Rework Rate ↓) × (Confidence Distribution ↑)

**If You Remember One Thing:** Systematic sparring transforms AI from an oracle delivering answers into a partner strengthening judgement. That distinction determines whether AI elevates or erodes organisational intelligence.

**Where This Takes You Next:** Sparring establishes the discipline of challenging AI outputs. But what happens when logic conflicts with intuition, or when data says one thing, but your gut says another? Next, we consider how to integrate AI partnership with human judgement.

CHAPTER 3

# GUIDED DECISIONS TO BALANCE WISDOM AND SPEED

# *Avoid full throttle without a compass*

⚖ ⚖ ⚖ ⚖ ⚖

*'Use your head. Listen to your heart. Follow your gut.'*

I've heard that advice all my life.

This year I had to live it, but realised that the order was also critical.

For decades I made decisions I could logically defend. My strength was analysis: examining options, weighing trade-offs, choosing the rational path. Teams trusted my judgement because I listened, assessed, and collaborated to agree on a balanced course. Motivated teams, quality results, and promotions followed.

My past successes had built a formula that felt reliable, a winning horse I kept riding, so I pushed forward despite always being under pressure. Then suddenly, I stopped. Not by choice.

The career that had defined my rhythm ended. Instinct from three decades in consulting kicked in: act, find the next role, rebuild fast, prove relevance. Within weeks, I had offers including funding for a start-up. Every option made logical sense — yet felt wrong.

I couldn't articulate why. My head said, *'These are good opportunities.'* Habit said, *'Keep moving.'* But my gut was whispering something speed made hard to hear.

I realised I wasn't short of options. I simply needed to realign with my purpose. So, I did the least logical thing: I paused. Six months to think, write, and reconnect with purpose before deciding what came next.

I didn't know it would become this book. I only knew that every fast, rational option felt incomplete, and ignoring that would be choosing efficiency over integrity.

## The Irony

I thought pausing would be the hard part. What I didn't anticipate was how writing this book would test whether I truly meant it.

Six months. That was my commitment. The business leader interviews started revealing insights I'd anticipated. Stories across industries began to flood in to support the one I had planned. With AI tools, I could synthesise years of writing and dozens of interviews almost instantly. My deadline seemed achievable.

I pushed forward, believing my deadline was the goal. I even started saying no to publishers who couldn't meet my strict timing.

I was doing exactly what I'd tried to avoid: running at full speed without asking if the destination was the right one. The irony wasn't lost on me. I'd rejected perfectly good job offers because they felt disconnected from purpose. Now I was rushing to hit an arbitrary deadline because... why exactly? To prove I could deliver on time? To show my pause was 'productive'?

When I finally listened to my gut, it said: 'You're writing a book about human leadership in the AI era, but allowing external factors to set your pace.'

The book took longer than expected. Financial pressure intensified. But the work became what it needed to be: an exploration of what leadership actually requires when machines can think faster than you can.

This wasn't just about the deadline. It was understanding that speed pretends to be your friend, especially when AI acceleration makes everything feel possible. But the moment where analytical clarity, emotional consequence, and instincts connect — that's where different decisions happen.

## Decision-Making: Speed, Not Shortcuts

Leaders know that good decisions blend analysis, values, and instinct. Under AI speed, however, applying the appropriate blend, and even any blend at all, can be difficult in the heat of the moment.

Drawing on insights from Amit A. Sidhpura, a Global Business Strategy leader at IBM, I revisited the classic 'head, heart, and gut' framework to make it more practical for leaders under pressure. In today's complex environment, simplicity matters, so I distilled it into two actionable centres, with the gut as the vital bridge connecting thought and emotion into decisive, coherent action:

### The Human Decision Sequence – with AI as Amplifier

Guidance → Gut → Head, with AI as Amplifier

**GUIDANCE CENTRE (Heart)**
*"Is this the right thing to do?"*
- Purpose & values
- Human consequences
- Direction before motion

**GUT SIGNAL (Bridge)**
*"Do I have the courage to act?"*
- Alignment / misalignment
- Converts direction into conviction
- Pattern recognition under pressure

**ACTION CENTRE (Head)**
*"How do we do this effectively?"*
- Frames the questions AI helps answer
- Executes with coherence
- Turns intent into action

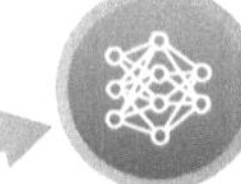

**AI (Amplifier)**
- Tests assumptions
- Reveals patterns
- Expands perspective

*External capability – not a decision centre*

**COHERENT ACTION**
Complete decisions under pressure

**Guidance** sets direction → **Gut** tests alignment → **Action** delivers coherence – with AI to test, not replace.

Coherent decisions come from integration, not speed.

The order of this approach matters. It should start with Guidance, then with Gut, and finally Action. Reverse the order, and the result is always *full throttle without a compass.*

Many failures happen when our urge to Action pushes us without correct Guidance. On the contrary, successes typically happen when a deep-rooted Guidance powers and directs the Action.

AI has become a disruptor for every leader. It offers faster analysis, deeper logic, and instant synthesis. Yet that abundance tempts us to bypass the moment where logic meets consequence, where data meets values, and speed meets wisdom.

When the Guidance Centre sets direction, the gut gives the signal, and the Action Centre does what it does best (framing challenges, designing tests, surfacing evidence, deciding) without violating what makes your organisation human.

Integration isn't optional anymore. It's the difference between decisions that look smart and decisions that are complete.

## Why Integration Matters Now: The Neuroscience Reality

Neuroscience validates what great leaders have always sensed. Decision-making operates across distributed neural centres. Your brain processes logic through your central nervous system. Your heart influences emotional regulation and relational connection through its own neural network of approximately 40,000 neurons. Your gut signals instinct and core identity through over 100 million neurons communicating directly with your brain via the vagus nerve.

These are physiological realities, not metaphors.

But AI has fundamentally changed their relationship. When AI makes analytical capability abundant, competitive advantage shifts. The Action Centre function becomes commoditised. Everyone has equal access to analysis.

Exceptional leaders still use the Action Centre, but they dial up the Guidance Centre to build trust and navigate values, and their gut to act with courage and sense patterns where data can't.

This connects to Chapter 1 where roles are shifting from execution expert to orchestration leader, demanding different decision-making capabilities. Efficient sparring in Chapter 2 revealed why individual capability matters; now we connect with the integration.

Like me, many leaders feel overwhelmed when considering how to make effective decisions that balance AI's instant analysis and the increasing pressure to move quickly.

That's what this framework is designed to help. Not new leadership skills, but structured discipline for applying capabilities you already possess, despite AI acceleration trying to bypass them. Its simplicity helps you recognise that, under pressure, you must first check the source (guidance vs fear) before optimising execution (action).

## The Guidance Centre: Where Direction Originates

This is where 'Values' live, where 'We' thinking replaces 'I' thinking, where connection to something larger than ego resides. The Guidance Centre asks: What serves the collective? What builds trust and capability, not just delivers metrics? What aligns with values under pressure?

Amit reframes emotional intelligence in a surprisingly analytical way: "*I spend a lot of time looking at data. But then there was a point where I started to say, I don't look at my own data. I've got emotional data that I've never even analysed.*"

He began observing his emotions just as a business analyst observes trends. Which situations triggered anxiety? When did certain feelings repeat? What patterns emerged over time? "*It is beautiful when you are able to do your own emotional analysis.*"

Most leaders struggle to treat emotions as legitimate business intelligence. Your Guidance Centre generates data, including discomfort from misalignment, calm due to coherence, or anxiety that your analytical mind hasn't consciously processed.

One of the most critical leadership capabilities in the AI era will be the ability to tap into your Guidance Centre. It will become the currency of trust. As hierarchies flatten and decision-making is distributed, you cannot rely on formal authority anymore. You need to build influence through genuine connections, demonstrating care, and navigate the emotional complexity of transformation.

AI will never replicate your Guidance Centre function. It can analyse sentiment, but it will never feel it, because it doesn't hold values. When an AI recommendation is logical but feels wrong, it's your Guidance Centre that sounds the alarm.

Without the Guidance Centre, you optimise for efficiency whilst destroying what makes people want to work with you. You make analytically sound decisions that fracture relationships and erode cultures.

Amit describes what happens when leaders operate from disconnected Action Centres. "*When you're disconnected from your guidance centre, everything you do is 'I' based because you're stuck in the mind. The mind is great at being that action centre. But if the action centre is not plugged into the guidance centre, then it's going rogue.*"

When Action runs without Guidance, decisions accelerate but direction fragments. Speed increases whilst coherence collapses.

## The Gut: The Signal That Connects

Your gut provides instinctive safety signals, identifies anchors, recognises patterns, and mobilises courage. When something feels wrong despite good data, when you sense unquantifiable risk, when you know what you won't compromise regardless of pressure, your gut is signalling.

The gut isn't a third centre requiring separate integration. It's the bridge converting Guidance Centre direction into Action Centre conviction.

Your Guidance Centre might say, '*This decision serves the enterprise.*' Your Action Centre might confirm, '*The analysis supports this path.*' But if your gut signals discomfort, that's information telling you something doesn't balance.

The gut synthesises experience into pattern recognition faster than conscious analysis. It signals danger through discomfort or confidence through certainty. In the AI era, your gut becomes a competitive differentiator. When everyone has equal analytical capability, advantage shifts to leaders who can sense what data misses, who recognise patterns across domains AI cannot connect, who have the courage to override algorithmic recommendations when something fundamental feels wrong.

Without the gut signal, you hesitate despite having information. You follow recommendations lacking conviction. You drift towards whoever presents the strongest analysis rather than holding to principles that matter.

Amit describes the gut as your connection point: "*When you're connected to your guidance centre through your gut, you're connected to universal knowledge. You're not doing anything out of ego or fear. You're doing it from a place of clarity.*"

The gut asks: '*Do I have the courage to act on this guidance?*' That question isn't about bravery. It's about alignment. When Guidance and Action connect through the gut, courage follows naturally. When they don't connect, the gut signals something's wrong.

## The Action Centre: Where Execution Happens

This is cognitive work leveraging AI's power. It can frame hypotheses, run scenarios, read signals, and make decisions. AI excels at processing at scale and surfacing patterns. Your job is to frame the right questions and apply context that AI alone can't reach.

The Action Centre must manage your AI partnership to structure problems, ask the right questions, and apply processing power to the right challenges. It interprets what AI reveals through the lens of strategic objectives that AI doesn't understand.

Amit treats intuition as a legitimate data point, "*When I feel something, I log it like data, then I use AI to test it. 'Show me support tickets from the last 90 days where sentiment dropped after this change.' Then suddenly my feelings become correlated, and I can act with confidence.*"

Applying this principle is the equivalent of walking into a board meeting saying, *'I had a gut feeling, so I acted on it.'* Instead, you should say 'I knew something was misaligned, so I investigated, and AI helped us find the impact on user trust post-rollout. Here's the mitigation plan.'

Guidance raises the signal. Gut gives us the go signal. Action proves it.

Without the Action Centre, you're conceptual but not practical. You understand values but can't execute against them. You recognise patterns but lack tools to test whether they're signal or noise.

The Action Centre in the AI era isn't about having answers. It's about framing questions AI can help answer, then synthesising results with context only humans possess.

## The Pause: Opening Space for Integration

When AI compresses analysis to seconds, pausing feels counterproductive. That's precisely why it's essential.

Leadership coach Sally-Anne Airey teaches a simple reset: "*Pause, Focus, Breathe.*"

"*People talk about pause, without knowing how to. The pause is an act of self-compassion and compassion towards others. Particularly when you're triggered, just give it a moment. Notice the sensations in your body. These signals are your body's early warning system telling you something matters.*"

The pause, in essence, takes you out of the noise to a place where you can avoid immediate reaction due to fear or ego. It's reconnecting with purpose, and as Sally-Anne puts it, "*You start to align with something bigger than your immediate state. In a world of intense velocity and massive pressure, how are you going to relate to it? It's by enabling yourself to be centred within it. The pause creates space for integration before pressure forces premature commitment.*"

In practice, the pause only takes a minute. But that minute determines whether you act from fear or from guidance.

## The Guidance Minute: Integration in Practice

Before analysis, write one short line for each question. Sixty seconds each. Clarity first, speed second.

### **Question 1:** Why this path?

This activates your Guidance Centre. Not 'the data says so' (that's abdication), not 'AI recommended it' (that's outsourcing judgement). 'Why' means logic that survives scrutiny independent of who's making the decision.

Reflecting on my book-writing experience, extending the deadline serves readers better than speed serves my ambition. If my purpose is elevating human leadership in the AI era, then that demands depth over speed. I'm then aligned with my purpose.

### **Question 2:** What trade-offs am I accepting?

This deepens Guidance Centre awareness. Every decision optimises for something at the expense of something else. The Guidance Centre forces honest acknowledgement.

I had to trade publication speed for depth of insights. I also had to accept the financial pressures resulting from this focus on writing, believing a better reader outcome was the approriate trade-off.

**Question 3:** What won't change?

By activating your gut, you will hear what truth survives this decision, regardless of pressure to compromise. The principle remains non-negotiable even when circumstances tempt abandonment.

My non-negotiable for the book was presenting a holistic, balanced, and practical approach for leaders to understand the importance of people-first AI augmentation.

**Question 4:** Where do I need to push back?

This activates the Action Centre. When do you override AI data? Where does analysis miss the core purpose? This is where your judgement becomes irreplaceable.

Whilst editing this book, I would ruthlessly cut content more suited to 'consulting' than practical application, regardless of effort invested.

This is like awakening the heart before the mind takes over, to protect judgement from being hijacked by urgency.

## Integration Under Pressure

Keith O'Loughlin, CEO of Everlough Holdings, an investment management business, faced a decision in which every analytical measure indicated that he should automate. His hardware reseller business, operating since 1993 with loyal customers and consistent revenue, was manual and relationship-intensive.

The pressure to scale through AI-enabled automation was intense. But Keith integrated Guidance, Gut, and Action to reach a decision that preserved value whilst acknowledging constraints.

### Guidance Centre: The Relationship Reality

Keith's Guidance Centre surfaced what spreadsheets missed. Customers weren't buying hardware. They were buying relationship confidence.

*"If you need a thousand laptops, two hundred screens, whatever, you ring our guys and they get it delivered. Customers love us. They feel the human element. It's very easy to kill that with AI."*

This wasn't a refusal to innovate. It was recognition that customers experience the business emotionally, not just transactionally. Remove the emotional connection, and you're competing on commodity pricing where margins compress.

His Guidance Centre also considered employees who'd built institutional knowledge about customer preferences, timing needs, and unspoken expectations. Automating expertise away might gain short-term efficiency but would lose what made the service valuable.

## Gut Signal: Pattern Recognition

Keith's gut brought pattern recognition from watching companies destroy brands through premature automation. "*When you kill a brand, you can't come back.*"

Too many people make decisions without listening to their instincts. Many spend their life living in their head, but to activate your gut, you must listen really hard to understand the nuances.

Keith also articulated why gut becomes increasingly critical as AI advances. "*Let's say you and I are running two separate companies. We now have the same playing field. Your analysts aren't better than mine because we both have AI. Over time, we both level out except when it comes to the gut stuff. AI can't do this, and life is still about people, so it's going to become a huge differentiator.*"

The gut asked, '*What feels wrong here despite good analysis?*' The answer was that automation would solve a growth problem by creating a value destruction problem.

Keith's gut also held identity clarity. This business was fundamentally a concierge service. That identity wouldn't survive standardisation purely for efficiency gains.

## Action Centre: Selective Execution

The analytical logic was compelling: automation would reduce costs, standardise margins, and scale infinitely. Every simulation supported the decision.

But Keith used his Action Centre to frame the problem correctly: "*Can we grow this business through automation without destroying what makes it valuable? Not 'Should we automate?' because that's lazy thinking.*"

His Action Centre also recognised that hardware is a commodity, and competitors could replicate technology instantly. The analytical advantage from automation would be temporary at best.

## The Integrated Decision

Keith eventually chose selective automation with AI handling logistics where efficiency matters, but human judgement staying in the loop where relationship value builds. The concierge model remained the anchor. Growth constraints were accepted in exchange for brand protection. "*There's a huge risk of eroding margins if we automate what's essentially a concierge business. People feel the heart of the business. I don't want that to be lost.*"

This is integration in practice. Guidance Centre maintained focus on customer experience, thereby creating loyalty, and on employee expertise, creating service quality. Gut recognised the pattern of efficiency destroying differentiation and signalled that the compromise shouldn't be made. Action Centre executed selective automation, preserving what mattered.

Keith's business decision mirrors my career and book decisions. Different stakes, different timescales, but the same integration principle. He had pressures where automation made logical sense. I had pressures that would be relieved by finishing quickly. Keith chose to preserve what customers valued. I chose to preserve purpose.

When analysis becomes abundant, judgement becomes scarce. Integration creates a human competitive advantage.

## Your Decisions Carry Your Fingerprint

When you make decisions purely from the Action Centre, you suppress uncertainty and ignore values, tension, and gut warnings. That suppression becomes an organisational pattern, and teams sense the anxiety you're masking. They mirror the panic you're projecting, and your unresolved chaos becomes their operating reality. I know this reality, as do many of the teams I have lead!

Your fingerprint is always present, but knowing whether it's applied consciously or unconsciously is the key. Deliberate integration makes it conscious.

Amit articulates this eloquently, "*Your inner world, those disruptions and suppressed emotions: these are your fingerprint. Each aspect you touch carries it.*"

That was my career crossroads. Analysis said, '*Take the job*,' but the emotions like anxiety and disconnection were business intelligence I couldn't ignore. Granting myself permission to treat discomfort as a signal was not a weakness; it revealed a misalignment my analytical brain couldn't yet articulate.

Fingerprints travel. Integrated decisions create coherence others can feel; fragmented decisions export confusion. The completeness you build within yourself becomes the coherence others follow. Chapters 4–6 show how personal integration scales into team trust and enterprise flow.

## AI + Human Partnership: The Sweet Spot

This is where human judgement and machine capability truly compound. The Guidance Centre sets direction. The gut adds conviction. AI tests and quantifies. The Action Centre executes, and together they create decisions neither could reach alone.

Keith applies this systematically, "*When my instinct conflicts with analysis, I don't dismiss either. I use AI to investigate what my gut detected. Sometimes, AI reveals data patterns that explain the unease. Sometimes, the investigation shows my instinct was responding to outdated patterns. Either way, this combination produces better decisions than choosing Action OR Guidance.*"

Each plays its part:

- **Guidance Centre:** anchors values and weighs human consequences
- **Gut:** surfaces misalignment and converts direction into conviction
- **AI:** processes at scale and pressure-tests hypotheses
- **Action Centre:** frames questions and interprets outputs

A simple self-check to close: '*Am I using all areas or am I letting one run the show?*'

## When Integration Feels Impossible

My resistance to integration has always been time pressure. Crises demand immediate response. Competitors move faster. Stakeholders want decisions now. Taking time to pause feels like a luxury you cannot afford.

But this is precisely when integration matters most.

Amit explains, "*When things go wrong, instinct kicks in, and you won't take time for a meaningful minute. You will just follow the state of mind you are in, and that's often stress or panic.*"

Under pressure, fear drives speed. Decisions happen fast, but consequences compound slowly. You've optimised for urgency but sacrificed wisdom.

Keith articulates the same principle, "*Constantly consuming information is like loud music that stops you from thinking clearly. AI can either amplify the noise or give you the silence needed for better decisions.*"

Use AI to create space for integration by handling analytical work that used to consume time needed for reflection.

When I left my role, integration felt like a luxury I couldn't afford. Financial pressures were real. Each day 'lost' felt like wasted time, but the integration moment was the decision: not choosing between specific opportunities but understanding where I was going. My Guidance Centre could assess values alignment. My Action Centre could evaluate each option analytically. But only my gut could tell me that accepting any of them would be choosing security over purpose, and that I'd spent my career making exactly that trade-off.

The pause didn't cost me opportunities, but it revealed that they were the next version of the same pattern I needed to break. That's what integration does under pressure. You should never fear a pause, especially when the benefit is that it prevents full throttle in the wrong direction.

Integration doesn't guarantee perfect outcomes. But it guarantees complete decisions.

I may have chosen the harder path. Perhaps I should have taken a job offer and written during weekends. I'm certainly poorer. But I will never regret choosing clarity over comfort. I have calm I've not experienced in years. I feel fulfilled. I'd rather fail having made a complete decision than have temporary 'success' whilst running from myself.

Your integration doesn't remove risks. But it ensures you're taking risks aligned with who you actually are.

## Building Integration Capability

Integration is a state you cultivate through deliberate practice. The four-week structure below is a progressive practice for developing a new operating state. "*You need to experience that state because up until you experience it, you can't really guide others,*" Amit explains.

### **Week One:** Observe Your Pattern

Track three decisions using the simple framework: What is my Guidance Centre saying? What is my gut signalling? What is my Action Centre executing?

Most leaders discover they consistently override certain signals. The pattern reveals which centre you've suppressed. Some leaders never consult Guidance, running purely on Action autopilot. Others have strong Guidance but weak Action, knowing what matters but unable to execute. Still others ignore gut signals, dismissing discomfort as weakness.

The observation week reveals your default pattern. You can't change what you can't see.

### **Week Two:** Force Integration

Choose one decision each day in which you deliberately pause before deciding. Use the four Guidance Minute questions. Don't just answer them mentally. Write them down.

Integration requires articulation, not just contemplation. The act of writing forces clarity. You cannot hide from incomplete thinking when you're staring at it on paper.

Notice where this feels uncomfortable. That discomfort is information. If writing about trade-offs feels exposing, you've been hiding costs from yourself. If articulating what won't change feels difficult, you haven't clarified your principles. If identifying where to push back creates anxiety, you've been avoiding necessary conflict.

The discomfort shows where growth is needed.

### **Week Three:** Test Under Pressure

Deliberately apply integration during higher-stakes decisions. Notice what breaks down when pressure increases.

Do you revert to Action-only decisions? Does Guidance disappear? Does gut get dismissed? The breakdown reveals where capability needs strengthening.

This is where integration stops being a technique and starts becoming an operating system. Under pressure, you'll default to what's most developed. If Action Centre is strong but Guidance is weak, pressure will amplify that imbalance.

The test week surfaces which centres need development.

### **Week Four:** Operate in an Integrated Way

By week four, integration shouldn't feel like a technique you're applying. It should feel like a state you're operating from.

Decisions start to flow. Misalignment surfaces naturally. You notice when Action races ahead of Guidance without needing to consciously check. Your gut signals register as information, not noise.

Integration becomes your default, not your exception. This is where capability compounds. Each integrated decision strengthens the next. The state becomes self-reinforcing.

This four-week practice isn't linear. Some leaders need longer. Others can compress it. What matters isn't speed. It's the integrity of development. Rush without reflection, and you'll build technique without transformation.

## What Integration Unlocks in You

Reflecting on my own decision to pause rather than return to a similar role, this wasn't the easy decision. The pause cost me months of income and momentum and added plenty of doubt, pressure, uncertainty, and risk.

But by connecting all three centres: my logic, grounding purpose, and instinct, conviction replaced doubt, and curiosity replaced fear. The process became honest and without regret. I found a peace and coherence that turned a hard decision into a complete one.

With complete decisions, you stop second-guessing: you know not just what you chose, but why. Teams feel this alignment, and integrated leaders project calm without hiding uncertainty. People sense when logic, values, and instincts align. They respond with trust.

The balance this brings has the additional benefit of helping make mistakes visible sooner and accelerating recovery. When trade-offs are made consciously, misalignment becomes information, not failure. Action-only decisions hide cracks until they widen. Integrated decisions, by contrast, surface tension early and allow repair. You combine AI's analytical precision with human synthesis. That combination becomes your sustainable edge.

My clarity became this book and alignment with who I am.

*'Use your head. Listen to your heart. Follow your gut.'*

I started this chapter with that advice. I thought I understood it, but I was wrong.

My sequence had been backwards. Action first, thinking second, feeling last. Speed over clarity, with pressure drowning out purpose.

The sequence that actually works:
**Listen to your heart. Trust your gut. Then use your head.**

Guidance first. Courage second. Execution third.

That reordering changed everything for me. It turned speed into clarity, pressure into purpose, and action into conviction.

This isn't slower leadership but complete leadership. The kind that holds under pressure. The kind AI cannot replicate.

Fast decisions have their place, but integration is what makes those decisions complete.

## The SPAR Integration

This chapter sits within Partner for a reason. You cannot meaningfully partner with AI or amplify through others if your own decisions lack integration. To achieve the completeness that speed tempts you to bypass, integration ensures your logic, values, and instincts align. When that coherence is visible, trust follows.

As Keith puts it, *"I'm not making fewer decisions or slower decisions. I'm making complete decisions. My analysis remains rigorous, but it's bounded by clarity of values and informed by instinctive wisdom."*

That's the distinction between leaders who *survive* AI disruption and those who *thrive* through it. Machines may match your analytical power, but they can't replicate the integration that earns human trust.

The pause will give you clarity.

Integration is the foundation for both trust and speed. Master it within yourself, and you can orchestrate it across teams and systems.

Your fingerprint travels. *Make it coherent.*

## Practical Application: Your Next Decision

Choose one real decision this week.

Pause first. Ask: Am I deciding from Guidance, or from speed?

Run the Guidance Minute (4 questions, 60 seconds each). Reconnect, then decide.

Capture it on one page: what we chose, why now, trade-offs, signals to watch, owner, next step.

Notice how clarity changes the conversation. That's integration working.

### Ritual: Daily Guidance Minute (90 seconds)

Before one decision each day, pause and write one line answering: Why this path? What trade-offs? What won't change? Where do I push back?

**Metric:** Guidance-Before-Action Ratio

Track decisions made after the Guidance Minute vs decisions made under pressure without pause. Set a target and check again after a month.

**If You Remember One Thing:** When Guidance to Gut to Action (plus AI) is intact, speed becomes strategic rather than reactive. If you feel pressured to make decisions, that's your signal to reconnect. Then move fast.

**Where This Takes You Next:** Having strengthened your foundation and learned to partner effectively, you're ready to build the orchestration system. Use integrated decisions as you transform decision-making across human and artificial intelligence, creating operational advantage.

CHAPTER 4

# FROM FUNCTIONAL PILOTS TO ENTERPRISE VALUE

# *When decisions move faster than coordination*

Whilst leading a workstream on a major transformation project in the Middle East, I experienced coordination failure in real time. It was painful, but became an important lesson for me.

Each workstream independently prepared implementation plans. After a month of intense work, each delivered excellent presentations. Then a board member asked a simple question that still echoes: '*Have you even spoken to each other before today? Your process flows don't align, your systems aren't connected, and your tech stacks aren't consistent.*'

He was right. Weeks of individual teamwork instantly became worthless.

What haunts me about that moment wasn't the wasted effort. It was how obvious the failure looked in hindsight, yet how invisible it remained whilst we worked. Each team optimised brilliantly within their domain. Together, those optimisations cancelled each other out.

When functional excellence outruns cross-functional alignment, performance fragments. I've seen this destroy value repeatedly, and now AI accelerates this risk exponentially.

## The Coordination Tax Nobody Calculates

The Airbus A380 programme provides a more costly illustration. Multiple international design teams worked in parallel, each manufacturing excellent components. Unknown to each team, they were designing on slightly different versions of the same software. Only during attempted assembly did they discover that the specifications didn't match. Two years delayed. Six billion dollars written off....

What fear makes leaders tolerate misalignment this long? In my experience, it's the belief that coordination slows execution. Teams prioritise velocity over visibility, assuming alignment can be retrofitted later. By the time the collision surfaces, the rework cost exceeds the original investment.

Before AI, organisations could recover from coordination failures by extending timelines and increasing budgets. Now, when competitive windows compress to days and insights arrive before traditional governance begins, the consequences multiply. AI accelerates individual work. Unless aligned, that acceleration fragments the coordination rhythm of the whole.

Current research from McKinsey, MIT, BCG, and Gartner show that between 70% to 95% of AI transformations fail to deliver expected value due to people and culture barriers rather than technical issues. This means at best, 35% of technology implementations achieve ROI or deliver sustained value.

It's understandable that new technology takes time to implement well, but functions that independently experiment without coordination capability or enterprise vision will fragment rather than scale. The gap between functional success and enterprise value often comes down to coordination readiness — an organisation's ability to synchronise decisions, information, and execution at AI speed. As we will see in Chapter 10, the solution isn't less experimentation, but systematic coordination that enables learning to compound across boundaries.

Pete Jaworski, Head of People Data & Analytics at Maersk, experienced his own coordination challenge. The board needed precise visibility into workforce costs by function and location to make strategic decisions. The data existed, Finance had their numbers, HR had theirs, but they didn't reconcile.

Maersk's Finance systems use one hierarchical logic and reporting approach, whilst HR tracks hierarchy differently, producing different

FTE counts and employee costs. Each system is excellent within its domain, but they weren't designed to coordinate. *"Some might say there is a data quality failure,"* Pete explains, *"but actually it's an architectural mismatch between financial accounting logic and organisational reporting logic. Our role is to work out how to advise the board to make strategic decisions when your most accurate data sources don't fully reconcile."*

Data coordination is one of the greatest problems facing multinational organisations, especially those that have grown inorganically. Each acquisition brings legacy systems not designed to work with others. This might partially explain why frontier firms spring from nowhere and produce staggering results: they don't have antiquated systems that create layers of data complexity. Unlike legacy organisations built on silos, frontier firms architect integration by design. I appreciate that it's easier to build new rather than renovate old, but we should learn from those at the cutting edge and reshape accordingly. In working towards this goal, there is much we can do to prevent functional excellence from turning into compounding problems at scale.

## When Scale Meets Constraint

At 78,000 people globally in a regulated pharma environment, Michiel van Duin (Mich), Chief People Technology, Data and Insights Officer at Novartis, faces coordination complexity multiplied by both scale and constraint. *"In a regulated pharma environment, we can't just move fast and risk breaking things,"* he begins. *"Patient safety, data privacy, clinical trial integrity, and adherence to AI regulations aren't negotiable."*

Questioning how Novartis balance AI's promise of speed within this environment, he explained this is the core tension: *"Coordination becomes a question of enabling functions to experiment and innovate whilst still maintaining the governance that maintains compliance."*

This captures the leadership challenge many now face. Coordination capability is becoming the modern leader's differentiator. Your ability to choreograph across systems determines whether AI creates enterprise value or expensive fragmentation.

## When Coordination Works

At Rightmove, the UK's largest online property website, Mark Abraham, Head of Organisational Development, achieved what most organisations miss. IT was rolling out Copilot to half the organisation. The People team was handling an increasing number of manager requests for guidance on difficult conversations, performance discussions, and feedback delivery.

Siloed thinking would have kept these separate. Mark built an AI Conversation Coach that delivered results neither function could achieve alone: fifteen hours saved weekly for People business partners, sixteen hours saved each week for all business managers, and NPS (Net Promoter Score) averaging 8 to 10.

Technically, the AI implementation was straightforward. The cross-functional coordination challenge was not. HR owned employee experience, IT controlled AI infrastructure, Legal governed risk, Finance wanted efficiency metrics. Four functions, four optimisation priorities, one system.

Mark's reflection captures the reality: *"We didn't have a work architect. It was just me, so I just cracked on. But I knew I couldn't crack on in isolation. I had to make sure IT, Legal, and Finance could see their priorities embedded in what we were building, not bolted on afterwards."*

That coordination capability, achieving velocity whilst ensuring that alignment wasn't an afterthought, is what prevented the fragmentation that derailed both my Middle East project and Airbus.

## How Structure Helps

Through SPAR, we've seen 'Strengthen Leadership Identity' build trust. In 'Partner with Intelligence' we're developing AI capability and disciplined thinking that can orchestrate across silos. You're mastering the use of individual AI to make better decisions faster. We will soon get to 'Amplify Team Capability', where orchestration becomes enterprise capability, and coordination becomes even *more critical.*

Coordination multiplies impact, but only when individual excellence scales across the entire system.

AI transformations that I have seen fail do so for one of three reasons. Excellence isn't replicated, coordination lags behind AI speed, or conflicting priorities collide unnoticed until the crisis hits.

By design, functions optimise for their own specific metrics. IT accelerates deployment. Finance demands efficiency. Legal ensures compliance. HR protects experience. Each optimises brilliantly within their domain. Together, they create exactly the fragmentation AI was supposed to eliminate.

This is the discipline I now teach. Turning inevitable collisions into coordinated clarity before they escalate into costly crises.

Having observed these failure patterns impact multiple projects and companies, evidence shows there are three coordination behaviours that, when consistently applied, can make a dramatic improvement:

1. **Make your reasoning visible early**
   Don't start with 'What's your plan?', but with 'What outcome are you optimising for, and what constraints shape it?' Visible reasoning replaces assumptions with shared understanding, so it pre-empts potential collision by giving others something to align *with*, not react *against*.

2. **Interrogate your own logic before sharing**
   Treat preparation as an act of respect. Use AI sparring and peers as options to expose weaknesses, test edge-cases, and surface trade-offs. Coordination only fails when untested thinking meets reality, so leaders who challenge themselves will always be more prepared to *align* instead of *defend*.

3. **Confront differences as design inputs, not defects**
   When IT's drive for speed collides with Legal's insistence on control, that's not dysfunction, but system intelligence surfacing real constraints. Name the tension, quantify the trade-off, and design the decision logic together. Coordinated teams turn disagreement into *architecture*, not *argument*.

I call this Show-Solo-Share, and it's here to provide the missing discipline between strategic vision and coordinated execution.

## Show-Solo-Share: How Coordination Happens

The method starts with alignment on a single objective, then moves through three coordination phases that transform how functions work together.

## Align on the Single Objective (Quick Test)

The underlying premise is to agree on a single problem or ambition that every function can unite behind. What must be avoided at all costs is 'this is IT's objective', or 'it's HR's problem, so then we can resolve it.' Find *one* shared outcome.

Apply these three simple questions to define AI's role in the project:

**Automate**: *Can this task or process be automated?*

Rules + Low consequence + Easy reversal

Example: policy look-ups

Requirement: AI to respond directly with 100% accuracy

**Augment**: *Does it augment People?*

Judgement needed + Human accountable + Context matters

Example: manager seeking work-life balance support

Requirement: AI to surface options and escalate when individual context is required

**Elevate**: *Could it elevate potential?*

Pattern across cases + Reveals systemic issue

Example: AI flags 40% of work-life balance queries from one department, which shows a critical issue requiring leadership action

At Rightmove, Mark first established an understanding of what both functions were solving: '*How do we support managers more effectively?*' Without that single objective defined upfront, coordination turns into functions talking to each other with earplugs in.

Once aligned on the objective, we then need to consider how and where AI should be used in the solution. Ask questions like, '*Can elements run without human judgement?*', '*Do we require augmentation?*', or '*Can we use this data to elevate findings to systemic insights?*'

Applying this type of logical reasoning prevents the common coordination breakdowns that occur when deciding how to deploy AI. With a newly found shared objective and an agreed role for AI in the process (which can evolve later), only then can *Show–Solo–Share* begin. Here is a simple discipline that prevents coordination breakdown before it compounds:

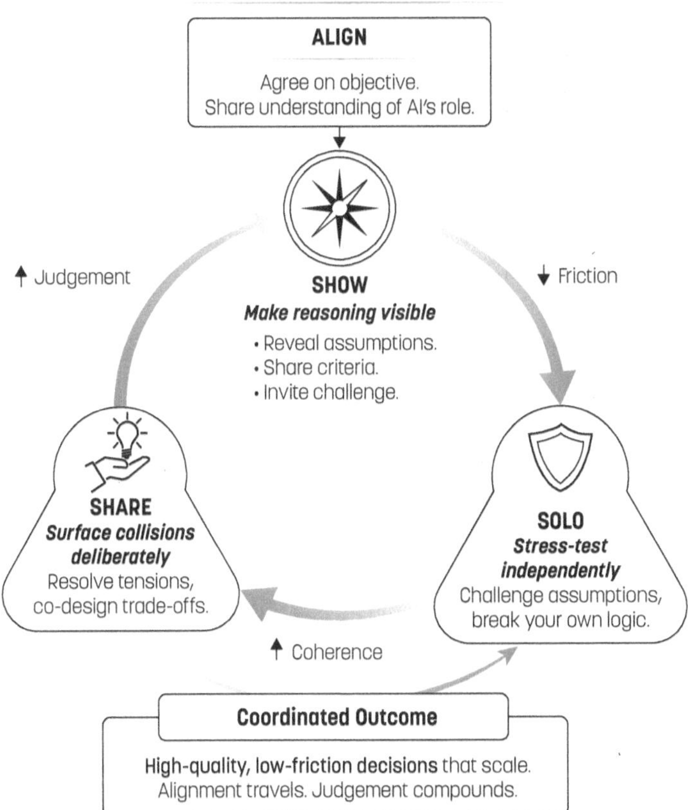


Turns functional tension into enterprise coherence

## **Show:** *Make Reasoning Visible*

Regretfully, I've learnt this lesson the hard way. Too often, I've said to my teams, *"Here's the plan, does anyone disagree?"* or focused on conclusions rather than the reasoning behind recommendations. That approach leaves assumptions hidden and conflict to surface later, usually as costly rework.

High-quality decisions depend on high-quality conversations, which means balancing clear assertions with genuine curiosity. As Amy Edmondson, the Harvard professor, explains, a simple prompt such as, "*What are we missing?*" can make all the difference and transform the tone of debate. Once leaders welcome bad news, treat red-status reports as signals, not failures, and thank colleagues for constructive dissent, safety will translate into performance.

This is the shift Amy defines: creating a healthy work environment where: *"Taking interpersonal risks, asking for help, admitting a mistake, or posing a difficult question, becomes expected and valued."* Crucially, she notes, *"This is not about being nice or lowering standards. These habits counter our unconscious bias to value agreeable voices more than challenging ones, and they create the conditions needed for the Show stage before decisions lock."*

Mark demonstrated this when IT proposed launching the platform to test, gather feedback, and to then iterate. *"Anything less than 100% accuracy means interactions may damage trust. With people's careers, mental health, and family situations at stake, we can't iterate our way out of that."*

By revealing his reasoning rather than defending a conclusion, he built alignment through understanding, not authority. IT wasn't wrong to propose their plan to iterate, as that is suitable for many applications, but Mark's visible reasoning clarified the shared goal of protecting employee experience.

This collision was not a failure but provided valuable information for better system-wide decisions. Pete applied the same discipline at Maersk: *"Our initial metrics focused on volume to assess productivity, with a clear understanding that quality measurement would follow. That transparency mattered because although our first analysis had limitations, it was a significant improvement over what we had before, and everyone knew how to interpret and act on those insights."*

Transparency prevents strategic decisions from being made on incomplete data. The coordination cost of visibility is minutes, and it can avoid months of rework after implementation. Making reasoning visible serves another purpose too: it exposes where you're uncertain, not just where you're confident. Those uncertainties signal where other functions may hold the insights you're missing.

It took me years to understand this principle. I'd often arrive at meetings with a plan and then present my polished recommendations. '*Here's what we should do,*' expecting colleagues to recognise the quality of my thinking and align accordingly.

Of course, they didn't always do that and would question or push back. Often objections would be raised that I'd already considered but just hadn't shared. In retrospect, I was creating the coordination failures I now want others to avoid. By showing conclusions without showing reasoning, I forced colleagues to either accept my authority or oppose my recommendation. There was no middle ground for genuine coordination.

*Your application:*

- *In your next meeting, commit to openly sharing the assumptions and criteria guiding decisions before making a final conclusion.*
- *Provide a space of safety so that others can raise hidden conflicts early to achieve better outcomes.*

## Solo: *Stress-Test Before Sharing*

After showing reasoning, each function should work independently to challenge its own thinking, and this is where Chapter 3's sparring can really extend capability.

Often, we arrive at coordination meetings unprepared, having rushed from one meeting to the next. Perhaps a reality, but this doesn't bring quality. Untested assumptions or knee-jerk reactions can be brought up without preparation or structured examination. Justified challenges may feel like an attack, and discussions can then become political rather than analytical.

The Solo phase changes that dynamic by forcing independent AI stress-testing before group coordination. Use your chosen tools to challenge assumptions, to ask for the strongest cases against your approach. Identify blind spots and try to break your logic.

AI surfaced considerations Mark hadn't initially examined. "*What if complex situations aren't clearly identifiable upfront? What if the policy database contains outdated guidance? What if managers game the system to avoid AI responses?*"

By stress-testing independently, Mark arrived at coordination meetings with examined thinking, not defensive positions. When others challenged his approach, he could acknowledge limitations he'd already investigated rather than treating questions as attacks.

Pete describes the same discipline, *"Before presenting an analysis to the board, I ask AI to identify what questions my analysis doesn't answer. Where could the CFO challenge this? Where would business leaders see gaps? That preparation transforms coordination from defending conclusions to exploring trade-offs together."*

*Your application:*

- *During all collaboration discussions, challenge your own thinking by sparring with AI to raise critical questions*
- *Try to identify blind spots, test edge cases, and anticipate objections*
- *Be better prepared to adapt rather than defend*

### **Share:** *Surface Collisions Deliberately*

After independent stress-testing, functions reconvene to share the examined reasoning. This is where conflicts can surface and be constructively resolved. At Rightmove, the Share session revealed genuine tensions. Before attempting to resolve the tensions, Mark returned to the Quick Test to see where the system could truly automate without quality risk, where augmentation required human judgement, and where they could elevate insights.

This shared logic prevented the coordination meeting from becoming a negotiation about preferences. The conversation shifted from '*who is right*' to '*where does each logic apply*'. IT achieved speed where automation carried no quality risk. HR maintained trust where human accountability mattered. Together, they uncovered systemic insights neither could reach alone.

*Your application:*

- *Run deliberate teaming conversations to surface conflicting priorities as insights (not dysfunctions).*
- *Guide the group to co-design trade-offs and decision logic that align with the shared objective rather than individual agendas.*

### When Adoption Hides Coordination Failure

One company I worked with had a total cost of deployment for an AI tool in the region of $10 million. The Technology team was celebrating the adoption metrics, as licence activation seemed to be tracking well. A year later, a senior leader asked for the ROI metrics, including understanding a list of top queries. The most frequent prompt was for the weather forecast, and the second was to generate cat pictures!

Usage metrics high, enterprise value ZERO.

A core goal of mine is to help teams shift from celebrating adoption as proof of impact. Enterprise value is not measured by how many people use a tool, but by the meaningful, coordinated outcomes achieved with it.

Pete's experience validates this: *"We have AI embedded into many of our tools. Many see it only as a note-taking time-saver, which of course it is, but there's a far greater business and customer impact we can have when we capture AI's full value. Without education and role models sharing the capabilities and benefits, it's hard to achieve this potential."*

A deeper challenge explains why adoption metrics can mislead. This echoes the 'invisible barrier' discussed in Chapter 1, where the issue isn't resistance but a gap in strategic connection and psychological safety.

Experienced leaders often resist AI adoption most strongly until they understand the compelling 'why'. They've spent years honing their knowledge, skills, and judgement, and for AI to become a true asset, they need to see it demonstrated as a tool that augments their hard-won expertise.

This is the moment to face the cultural challenge head-on. If using AI feels like admitting weakness or 'cheating' in a high-performance culture, it will remain hidden or resisted. The shift happens when top leaders role-model how AI elevates critical thinking and solves more complex problems, not merely saves time. Without that cultural signal and clear connection to high-value work, even the best tools remain underutilised.

This creates an orchestration paradox. Senior experts resist or wait for compelling use cases, whilst junior employees adopt AI tools readily, seeking ways to accelerate and optimise. When these groups operate at different speeds, the organisation fractures. Improvements occur in pockets and silos, whilst strategic, cross-functional wisdom lags behind.

Show-Solo-Share addresses this directly by making senior specialists demonstrate their methods, breaking the taboo through visible leadership. When experienced leaders show their AI-enhanced reasoning and openly display their learning process, they model judgement rather than control, building the psychological safety that transforms adoption from mere tool usage into genuine coordination. This is what organisational transformation requires.

Mich identifies another critical failure pattern that prevents pilots from scaling. *"Speed is great,"* he notes, *"but before experimenting, you need an understanding of what good looks like and a baseline. Otherwise, it's hard to go beyond the initial pilot and scale for enterprise value."*

The discipline comes in asking the right questions upfront, such as '*What's the baseline? What does success look like? What metrics will prove it?*' Mich stresses the fact you must: *"Set up proper systems and processes for A/B testing involving your end users to validate your experiment before you decide to scale. If you don't do this upfront, you limit success."*

This explains why over three-quarters of AI pilots fail to deliver value. Organisations skip the coordination foundations, baseline metrics, and clear problem definition, and instead rush straight to experimentation. The pilot succeeds within one function, but then fails when attempting to scale, because nobody established the cross-functional goals or even how to systematically measure success.

## Turning Coordination from Heroics into Advantage

At Novartis' scale, coordination becomes a systematic discipline, not heroic effort. Mich's philosophy is clear: *"AI replaces repetitive work, not workers, so our people can focus on higher-value, human judgement. When we automate administrative tasks, for example, scheduling events or interviews, summarising notes, creating task lists, and basic policy queries, we're not eliminating expertise; we're elevating our people to focus on the judgement calls that require their scientific knowledge and human insight."*

Mich's responsible AI frameworks become coordination mechanisms, not bureaucracy. *"We've built guardrails into our function's AI initiatives to ensure compliance with applicable laws and Novartis governance frameworks. Data ethics reviews, constant testing on our systems and processes, privacy safeguards, and legal assessment under the applicable AI regulations. But these aren't bureaucracy. They're coordination mechanisms."*

The result of this approach is clarity and velocity. When all teams operate within the same responsible AI framework, they can move faster because they're not creating compliance problems that require expensive remediation later.

The principle that intelligent coordination accelerates progress also equally applies to data and governance. At Maersk, Pete's vision echoes the same integration imperative:

*"AI is moving towards helping us solve fundamental issues within our data models. Bridging gaps between Finance and HR, to pull in operational performance metrics, commercial productivity, to connect disjointed systems, and to provide one consolidated version of truth. This consolidated data model will address the business intelligence the company needs to run things sustainably and intelligently."*

But Pete recognises sequence matters. *"There is a clear willingness to partner commercial and HR data to understand performance behaviours. The coordination challenge isn't technology; it's building the cross-functional analytical capability whilst data architecture evolves."*

Coordination capability must come before system integration. Show-Solo-Share builds the thinking discipline. The Quick Test provides the decision logic and together, they allow organisations to coordinate at AI speed before perfect systems exist.

When organisations move from functional pilots to enterprise value, the shift follows a consistent pattern:

| Pattern | Old Logic | Coordinated Logic |
|---|---|---|
| Functional pilots | Prove capability | Compound learning across the system |
| Adoption KPI | Usage counts | Enterprise impact |
| Local excellence | Fragmented wins | Systemic value |
| Decision velocity | Speed at any cost | Speed with alignment |
| Risk management | Control through hierarchy | Clarity through visibility |

Experimentation is not the problem; uncoordinated logic is. When functional metrics conflict, surface the collision immediately using Show–Solo–Share. Before committing, map your decisions and ensure judgement is applied where it matters most. Ask explicitly:

- Where can this run without human judgement?
- Where does human context materially improve the outcome?
- Where do strategic or ethical implications require leadership involvement before scale?

This is how organisations move fast without fragmenting, and how early AI momentum converts into durable enterprise value.

The coordination cost of pausing for this clarity is always lower than the rework cost of discovering functional incompatibility during implementation.

Mark's discipline demonstrates systematic coordination in practice:

A) Each function shows reasoning on pending AI decisions.
B) Solo stress-testing occurs with AI partnership.
C) When share session surfaces collisions, the quick test resolves them.

Pete suggests tracking coordination quality through leading indicators beyond adoption. Decision reversal rates. Cross-functional rework frequency. Time-to-alignment on contested decisions. *"When these metrics improve, we know coordination capability is developing, not just AI adoption."*

Coordination becomes systematic through discipline. The leaders who master this progression don't just perform better with AI they become essential to their organisations because they've built a capability that competitors cannot replicate through technology alone.

**Self-check:** How can you better surface a potential collision before it happens?

## Connection to SPAR

The progression from Partner to Amplify shifts from improving your decisions to coordinating decisions across functions optimising differently.

Show-Solo-Share extends capabilities you've already built. Strengthen taught you to make reasoning visible. Show extends that transparency across functions. Partner taught you to stress-test assumptions, Solo prepares that discipline for group coordination. Share creates the forum where optimisation conflicts surface and are resolved.

The coordination challenge is exponentially harder because your success now depends on others implementing decisions despite optimising for different outcomes. This is why we see such high failure rates in organisations mastering individual AI capability but falling short at coordinated implementation. Functional pilots typically optimise locally but often fail to elevate potential enterprise-wide.

Show-Solo-Share provides the missing discipline for coordination when AI enables individuals to move faster than traditional governance can coordinate.

## The Limitation Show-Solo-Share Reveals

This rigour offers a way to solve one of the hardest coordination challenges, to prevent collisions when functions optimise differently. But coordination alone doesn't guarantee strategic correctness. Alignment is powerful, but only if the goal is right.

Consensus can feel like validation, yet agreement doesn't always equal accuracy, which is why coordination capability must pair with strategic challenge.

Before alignment becomes execution, be the leader who asks: '*Are we optimising for the right outcome? Do shared assumptions deserve interrogation?*'

Create the discipline to align fast and transparently, then pair it with a systematic challenge to ensure you are both coordinated and focused on the right goal.

- **Ritual:** Weekly Show-Solo-Share
- **Show** the issue with shared facts and context.
- **Solo** articulate functional perspectives and constraints.
- **Share** a coordinated decision with explicit trade-offs.

Select one cross-functional challenge and run this weekly:

**Align:** Firstly, establish the single objective you're achieving together. Use the Quick Test to clarify where AI fits. Then apply the Show, Solo, Share principles.

This will build the muscle of horizontal coordination and the ability to coordinate without escalation.

**Metric:** Time from issue raised to coordinated decision with reasoning understood and accepted by all affected functions. Speed alone is not the goal. Shared understanding is.

**If You Remember One Thing:** Most coordination failures aren't caused by disagreement but by unspoken assumptions crossing boundaries unseen. The Show–Solo–Share discipline works because it makes those assumptions visible before they turn into friction, so when coordination improves, execution accelerates naturally.

**Where This Takes You Next:** We have strengthened horizontal coordination; next we introduce the missing dimension, which is vertical judgement alignment. We explore the AI Board Consult to better appreciate perspectives across decision levels.

CHAPTER 5

# THE AI BOARD CONSULT: FOUR VOICES FOR BETTER DECISIONS

# Be quick, don't hurry

*Humility isn't modesty — it's the confidence to admit your analysis might still miss something critical.*

A leader who has that awareness keeps decisions open just long enough to see what speed can sometimes hide.

We've all seen leaders make apparently 'smart' decisions that later destroy competitive advantage, damage culture, or trigger avoidable customer issues. At my previous consulting firm I experienced my fair share of these. Often, poor outcomes are explained away as the result of pressure, urgency, or having to make a call with incomplete information, but the truth is usually more subtle. In the pursuit of efficiency, speed, and simplification, systematic challenge gets skipped. Sometimes through overconfidence, but more commonly through fear that scrutiny will slow execution and in many teams, the people who see the risks first — often the most junior — feel least able to question Partner decisions.

This rhythm is predictable when stakes rise and calendars compress, not through ill intent, but expedience. It becomes easy to mistake clarity of data for clarity of direction. After all, your organisation needs decisiveness... Weeks later, the decision that looked right reveals costs you didn't see. The fundamental cause is speed outrunning judgement.

I learned this lesson by being aware of my tendency to move forward and skip the pause where broader consequences can surface. AI makes that temptation even stronger. Its instant, polished analysis makes slowing down feel unnecessary, but speed without challenge leaves you open to costly mistakes, weakened capability, broken trust, frustrated customers, and failed execution.

John Wooden's famous line for his UCLA team continues to be a warning for the AI era, *"Be quick, but don't hurry."* The distinction matters. Quick is decisive with systematic challenge. Hurry is rushing without thought. The difference isn't the speed but the process. Done correctly, a systematic challenge won't slow decisions but will help prevent the expensive reversals that eventually slow progress.

This chapter introduces an additional discipline to balance speed with systematic challenge.

## Why the Pause Matters More Than Ever

Harvard Business Review found 97% of 10,000 senior leaders believe strategic thinking is critical for future success. However, with the leaders I work with, few practice it systematically, usually because of time pressure and a lack of simple methods to handle complexity and uncertainty.

Andrea Petrone works with CEOs navigating strategic inflection points. He describes the current boardroom reality plainly, *"The level of uncertainty and ambiguity at the top table is increasing exponentially, not incrementally. Mounting external factors are making sound decision-making incredibly difficult. CEO tenures are shortening from six or seven years down to three or four, and as a result, time for impact shrinks, whilst pressure increases."*

Under pressure, leaders often default to efficiency logic to relieve the demand for fast results within compressed timeframes. I repeatedly experienced this in Big Consulting with senior leaders far removed from 'actual work', simply looking at spreadsheets that seemed defensible. But in the end, what gets sacrificed is the strategic depth that creates sustainable advantage, the long-term capability development, the trust-building, and the execution reality that doesn't show up in spreadsheets.

In Chapter 4, you built coordination capability through Show-Solo-Share. In this chapter, we extend that discipline to high-stakes decisions where speed and scrutiny must coexist.

## AI Board Consult: Four Voices of Strategic Decision-Making

Many well-intentioned leaders repeatedly make fast decisions that look 'smart' yet can destroy potential. Financial efficiency typically dominates discussions whilst other critical perspectives are ignored or dismissed.

The challenge isn't a lack of leadership intelligence. Under pressure, it's natural to collapse complex decisions into manageable analysis, but this can miss other essential voices that aren't just stakeholder perspectives but strategic questions that force perspective beyond immediate urgency. To solve this frequent challenge, I developed the AI Board Consult discipline to transform isolated decisions into orchestrated wisdom by forcing leaders to examine blind spots before committing to action. The four voices are:

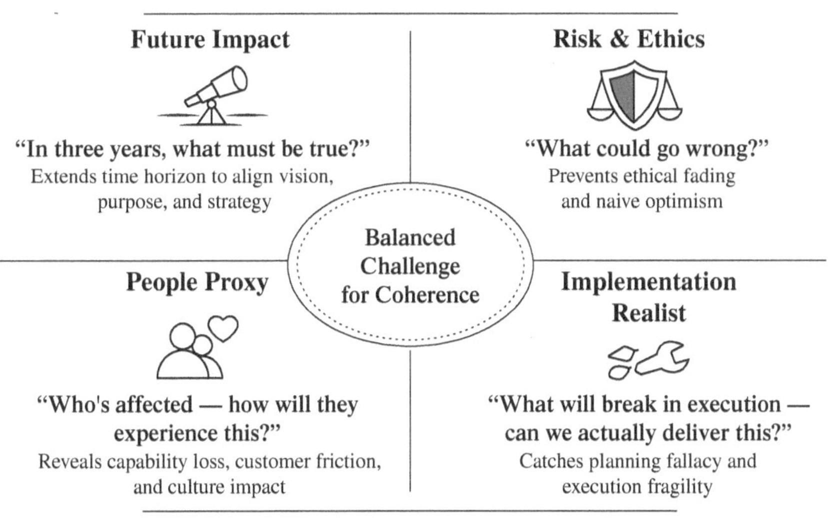


**Four voices. One decision.**
**Prevent blind spots in AI-accelerated decisions.**

Before deep diving into each voice, let's first consider the risks of myopic thinking that ignores these four voices, or any other voice other than your own.

## The WeWork Lesson

The WeWork story may be known to some readers, but it's generally cited as a governance failure. Yet the board had diverse expertise, which shows the issue wasn't knowledge but the absence of intrinsic challenge discipline. No voice was assigned to question whether hypergrowth itself was the right strategy, what happened when growth stopped, or whether operational complexity would break execution at scale. All four voices were absent, which is precisely why the failure was so catastrophic. WeWork collapsed from a $47 billion valuation to bankruptcy between 2019 and 2023, with the loss of 4,000 jobs.

Founder Adam Neumann controlled WeWork through supervoting shares: ten votes per share, compared to one vote for other investors. This essentially gave him absolute board control, even as the company was haemorrhaging money in the pursuit of aggressive growth.

If WeWork's board had forced systematic voices into decisions, they would have realised hypergrowth was not sustainable, recognised clear conflicts of interest, validated the voice of the people, and verified execution capability.

No single team can have perfect foresight, but improvements happen through disciplined examination, ensuring different time horizons, stakeholder impacts, and execution realities are heard before commitment locks in.

## When Efficiency Logic Meets Capability Reality

Antonio Calco' Labruzzo, Senior Vice President People and Culture at Arcera Life Sciences, faced a decision that will feel familiar. One of his past teams was designing AI-driven reporting automation across a complex global business. The efficiency case was compelling; they could eliminate manual reporting cycles, reduce FTE requirements, and accelerate decision-making for executive leadership.

*"Initially, there was a temptation to automate everything so that the CFO only saw a smart dashboard, but never the background reports. Full automation across multiple countries would significantly reduce cycle times. Everything looked positive on the first review."*

This is what I call the 'acceleration trap', where AI speeds up decisions and makes blind spots harder to notice — and even harder to articulate.

For example, you can analyse workforce data, financial projections, and operational metrics to optimise restructuring. But in doing so, you risk ignoring what data can't show: trust, expertise development, innovation capability, and the human dynamics that drive performance.

Under pressure, leaders naturally default to behaviours that collapse decisions to rapid logic, but in doing so, sustainable advantage is often sacrificed. Andrea Petrone's field observation with CEOs validates this pattern: *"I regularly watch senior leaders skip robust discussions about future impact and trade-offs with people inside and outside the organisation. These conversations require acknowledging uncertainty and long-term consequences, but under quarterly pressure, they feel like a luxury. Then six months later, the realisation hits that the required expertise has been automated away."*

The four voices provide a structure to balance speed with systematic challenge.

## The Revelation of The Four Voices (Appendix C)

Each voice catches different categories of bias that are amplified under pressure. To catch these biases, applying dedicated voices forces alternate perspectives into the decision process.

Having witnessed many failures, I recognise that, no matter how rigorous someone's thinking, there are always blind spots shaped by the outcome being prioritised at that moment. Andrea describes the prerequisite for effective AI partnership, *"You can't see blind spots without asking great questions that elevate above the details. Leaders need a helicopter view founded on depth of reasoning. Peter's approach provides that helicopter view with systematic reasoning."*

## Future Impact: Extends Your Horizon

It asks: '*What's the true cost of this choice over twenty-four months, including capability development, competitive positioning, and whether short-term efficiency creates long-term disadvantage?*'

The Future Impact perspective forces you beyond quarterly thinking and immediate efficiency gains. It catches current *bias*, the tendency to prioritise immediate benefits over long-term costs because today feels urgent, and the future is abstract.

In Antonio's case, the Future Impact challenged: '*What happens to career development when we eliminate the analytical work building expertise? In 18 months, will our finance team have the critical thinking muscle to provide insights AI can't generate? What analytical capability do we lose if we remove country CFOs from the interpretation process?*'

Nobody had asked these questions during efficiency planning. The spreadsheet showed FTE reductions and cycle-time improvements. It didn't show capability erosion or long-term competitive damage. This voice caught Antonio when potential gains looked compelling but would have created capability gaps, damaging competitive positioning over time.

## Risk & Ethics: Protects Your Integrity

It asks: '*What could go wrong, and would we be proud of how we handled the human consequences? Not just compliance risk, but reputation, trust, and societal impact.*'

This voice catches **ethical fading**, the gradual erosion of ethical considerations under operational urgency. Time pressure makes us treat values as negotiable rather than fundamental. Dedicated risk time ensures trust and accountability are designed into the process, not retrofitted after problems surface.

In Antonio's case, Risk & Ethics questioned: '*What happens to trust if leadership only sees AI-filtered dashboards? How do we maintain accountability when the interpretation layer disappears? Would we be comfortable explaining this approach to external stakeholders who question whether human judgement still informs strategic decisions?*'

The automation logic had focused on efficiency gains. This voice revealed governance and trust implications that would surface only after implementation, when reversal becomes expensive. Antonio's team ran standalone sessions where financial benefits were out of bounds, and only risk questions were permitted. Simple, effective, and clarifying.

## People Proxy: Reveals Human and Customer Impact

It asks: '*How does this land with the people who pay us AND the people who deliver for us? Who benefits, who pays the real cost, and is there a path that achieves the goal whilst preserving human potential?*'

This voice catches two related biases simultaneously:

**Productivity bias:** This refers to the assumption that efficiency equals progress, even when it weakens the capabilities that create future advantage. '*Does this elevate capability or quietly degrade it?*'

**Inside-out thinking:** This means optimising what's convenient for us whilst degrading what matters to customers. '*How does removing human interpretation affect our ability to respond to client needs that don't show up in standard metrics? What relationship intelligence do we lose?*'

People Proxy asked both external and internal questions in Antonio's case: '*How does removing human interpretation affect our ability to respond to client needs that don't show up in metrics? What message does automation send about value? Are we creating paths to higher-value work or just eliminating learning? What happens when teams stop engaging deeply with local business dynamics? What customer friction are we creating?'*

This tension exposes a deeper test of two *Conductor Capabilities*: Trust Stewardship and Enterprise Orchestration. When AI becomes the primary interface at work, the conditions for connection, collaboration, and trust fundamentally change. Andrea reflects on the consequences of this shift: "*The People Proxy is the most critical and complex. Imagine when people start working more with AI than with real people. Teamwork and collaboration conditions will fundamentally change, so we need to think through how people will connect, and this requires an entirely new leadership model. These conversations are not happening enough now.*"

When human interpretation is reduced, trust must be deliberately designed, and orchestration must ensure that context, meaning, and connection do not disappear in the pursuit of efficiency.

My question to you is, are you designing the conditions for teams to sustain shared understanding, sound judgement, and trust, so that insight and competitive advantage still emerge, even as AI becomes the primary interface?

## Implementation Realist: Tests Execution Truth

It asks: '*What might break in execution, especially the operational and behavioural elements we're not measuring? What's the gap between spreadsheet logic and organisational reality?*'

This voice catches planning fallacy, the optimism bias that assumes implementation will proceed as planned despite evidence that complex initiatives rarely do. It forces honest conversation about whether you truly have the capability to execute what you're committing to, or whether you're presuming capability into existence.

In Antonio's case, the Implementation Realist warned: '*What happens when the dashboard shows something unexpected and nobody understands why? What's our backup when automated processes break, and we've lost the expertise to fix them? Do we have the people, skills, and troubleshooting capability to actually deliver this, or are we building fragility disguised as automation?'*

This perspective revealed the human reality that elegant plans often ignore. The spreadsheet showed efficiency gains, but the Implementation Realist forced the question of whether they had the capability to troubleshoot if automation fails.

## Doubling Value Instead of Cutting Costs

Each voice revealed blind spots the efficiency case had missed. Together, the four perspectives showed a path Antonio describes as doubling the business value instead of just cutting costs.

The solution preserved human judgement whilst capturing efficiency gains. Automated systems generated integrated analysis, but humans added validation, insight, and strategic recommendations before submission to group leadership.

*"This kept essential human judgement and strategic discussion in the process and doubled the business value compared to pure cost cutting,"* Antonio reflected. *"We realised our initial approach would risk losing many critical benefits, including human insight and flexibility, what I call critical thinking in the chain."*

This demonstrates why systematic perspective-taking matters. The case for efficiency might be clear, and the dashboard colours are green, but when Antonio's team deliberately challenged their thinking through four distinct voices, they uncovered the competitive advantage of enterprise value rather than only cost-cutting.

*Your application:*

*I invite you to pause here for a* ***Meaning Minute.*** *Think through what the likely ROI might be if you spent one hour focusing on your next critical decision.*

- *Could this pause prevent a future decision reversal that would require months to correct?*
- *Could the coordination cost of systematic challenge be lower than the future cost of rework and failure?*

If the answer is yes to either question, block sixty minutes in your diary now.

## The Sixty-Minute AI Board Consult

Sixty minutes can feel expensive when your calendar is already packed, but don't think of this as taking time; think of it as investing time where returns will compound. This is a reframe to an investment with measurable returns.

This can work in three ways, so select what fits your situation:

1) **Solo preparation**: Use AI sparring to stress-test your thinking through each voice before bringing the decision to your team. This is particularly valuable for preparing high-stakes proposals where you need to anticipate challenges.
2) **Team meeting**: Assign each voice to someone who can authentically represent that perspective. The diversity of viewpoints creates the challenge that reveals blind spots efficiency logic misses.
3) **Hybrid approach**: When a critical voice is missing from the room, use AI to represent that perspective. Better to have AI simulate Future Impact or People Proxy than to make the decision without those questions being asked at all.

### **Separate:** 15 minutes

Work voice by voice. Under four minutes each without others interrupting. Capture only what this voice sees. Separation prevents economic frame dominance. Whether working solo with AI, assigning voices to team members, or using AI to fill gaps, the discipline remains the same: each voice gets dedicated time without interference from the others.

Set a timer, work through each in turn, and move on regardless of whether the conversation feels complete.

### **Integrate:** 30 minutes

Consolidate the four lists and name any collisions. The goal is clarity on what you're optimising for and what the acceptable consequences are. If you've done this alone, this is where you bring your stress-tested thinking to the team. If you've run this as a team, make sure different perspectives are voiced productively.

Either way, the integration phase is where leadership earns authority, ensuring every voice has been heard, all trade-offs are explicit, and the decision accounts for consequences you can name rather than discover expensively later. Watch for the pattern where one voice gets dismissed as 'slowing us down' or 'not understanding the urgency'. That's usually the voice catching the bias you most need to address.

If Future Impact feels like luxury thinking under time pressure, that's precisely when you need it most. If People Proxy seems sentimental when efficiency logic dominates, that's the signal that productivity bias is active and unchallenged.

### **Decide:** 15 minutes

Make your decision, then publish a single page documenting your choice, the reasoning behind it, acknowledged trade-offs, risks you're monitoring, the accountable owner, and when you'll review progress. The single-page discipline matters. If you cannot articulate your decision, its reasoning, acknowledged trade-offs, risks, accountable owners, and timings on one page, you haven't actually decided, but just postponed clarity until implementation forces it.

Immediately apply the changes to create active commitment and accountability, rather than just intentions. Shifting budgets, headcount, or timelines will immediately adjust people's understanding that this wasn't 'just another pointless meeting', but active decision-making.

Whether you've worked alone, in a team, or used AI to fill perspective gaps, the test is still the same: did the decision become something executable with clear accountability? AI is a thought partner enhancing human perspective, never a replacement for the judgement that makes decisions stick.

## Creating The Safety AI Can't Provide

The framework is effective only when the environment is safe to challenge compelling AI-generated analysis. Without psychological safety, dissent feels like a career risk. When algorithms validate the preferred path, silence becomes the default.

Andrea is clear about the conditions required, *"If transparency, openness, and authenticity exist in the boardroom, people have more opportunity to listen, reflect, and generate better ideas. AI will never replace that. Humans have an incredible power to generate insights if they are in the right condition to do so."*

When leaders are clear about what they expect and explicitly invite challenge, disagreement becomes professional contribution rather than career risk. The AI Board Consult creates that space, makes reflection non-negotiable and gives team members voice with accountability.

In our discussions, Harvard's Amy Edmondson captured this leadership imperative with precision, *"Many say 'Silence is free', but as a leader, your job is actually to make silence costly and voice free."* This single sentence captures the essence of this chapter. Systematic challenge can only happen when not only is it safe to speak up, but actually expected for people to question a dominant view. This applies both to people and for AI.

## Competitive Advantage Through Systematic Thinking

*"AI is already at the decision-making table. The real question is whether people still are,"* Antonio reflects. His experience proves systematic perspective-taking isn't risk management but competitive advantage creation.

*"When I applied systematic approaches, they weren't sentimental or administrative, but pivotal and strategic. Sustainable performance comes from trust, capability, and human judgement, things no algorithm will replace."*

The four voices ensure decisions build rather than erode human capabilities, creating lasting advantage. Organisations develop the capability to make deliberate, informed choices that compound into a sustainable market position.

This isn't slowing decisions but accelerating learning by stress-testing before failure.

Consider the pattern: A decision is made in haste, then implementation begins. Three months later, complaints surface about impacts nobody anticipated. Six months later, the decision gets revised. Nine months later, you arrive at the point that a sixty-minute upfront challenge could have avoided.

Organisations that embed this discipline don't just make better decisions. They build capabilities that competitors cannot replicate through technology alone. Your competitors can buy the same AI. They cannot buy the disciplined thinking that makes AI serve judgement rather than bypass it.

*Your Application:*

*Run the sixty-minute AI Board Consult on your next significant decision. Start with the voice you usually skip. For smaller decisions twelve minutes may be enough, i.e. three minutes per voice. In my experience, applying all voices always uncovers something new.*

*Track whether this practice helps you reduce future decision reversals.*

**If You Remember One Thing:** The perspective you instinctively skip is usually your greatest blind spot. Sixty minutes of disciplined scrutiny before commitment prevents months of corrective effort afterwards.

The acceleration trap is real. AI speeds both decisions and their consequences, so taking a systematic perspective ensures that speed serves judgement rather than bypassing it.

**Where This Takes You Next**: You have strengthened decisions at the point of commitment, but many leadership challenges only emerge when decisions travel across teams, functions, and systems, particularly whilst under pressure and with incomplete information. We now shift to sustaining judgement and coherence as decisions scale across the enterprise.

CHAPTER 6

# EVOLVING THE ART OF STRATEGIC DECISIONS IN THE AI ERA

# *Judgement and orchestration under pressure*

## When Speed Meets Complexity

Strategic decisions in the AI era demand a judgement paradox: leaders must lead with AI's analytical power whilst staying human in their judgement and values. Up to this point, you've built capability step by step, strengthening thinking with AI, sparring, integrating logic, purpose and instinct, and making trade-offs visible whilst leading with disciplined curiosity.

These practices sharpen individual judgement, but the challenge now shifts to preserving that quality as decisions move through the enterprise at speed.

Robust decision-making has never been trouble-free, but AI now appears to make it deceptively easy. Confident outputs can create the illusion of certainty, whilst sound judgement still requires scrutiny. The defining challenge for modern leaders is sustaining coherence under the constraints of acceleration and ambiguity. As speed increases, it becomes easier for logic, purpose, and instinct to drift apart.

You have learned how to pause and surface assumptions; now the task is translating that discipline into movement. Hesitate too long and opportunities vanish — move too fast and errors multiply before they can be corrected.

This is where individual capability must evolve into enterprise rhythm.

At the enterprise level, AI has transformed how information is accessed and analysed, but not how decisions are made. Processing complexity has never been easier, but maintaining meaning, accountability, and alignment remain a human responsibility.

This tension plays out across all industries and large organisations. At ABB, strategy and finance teams shifted from annual planning to 90-day forecasting cycles, analysing millions of data points across twenty-five segments and one hundred countries. The advances made possible by AI are clear, but the criticality of human judgement is greater than ever. As Massimo Muzzi, VP Strategy & Sustainability in the electrification business, explains, "*Without AI, we'd need hundreds of analysts to produce the same results. But even now, the final decisions are still human.*"

Massimo adds, "*The harder part isn't analysis anymore; it's maintaining coherence at the same speed the data arrives. Leadership judgement must move just as fast, or we lose the link between insight and execution.*"

His observation captures a central theme: better analysis does not guarantee better alignment. The real test is sustaining judgement quality and coherence whilst operating at high speed.

## Scaling Strategic Decision-Making

This is where the transition from Partner to Amplify becomes critical. You've built personal capability with AI and strengthened trust within your team. Now, those capabilities must scale across the enterprise, where strategic decisions travel through multiple functions, time zones, and technologies.

AI has changed the nature of strategy itself. Decisions that once unfolded over months now compress into days. Insights arrive faster than organisations can absorb them. The challenge is no longer *access to information* but *maintaining coherence* as information multiplies.

In this environment, leadership becomes a test of rhythm, knowing when to slow for reflection and when to accelerate for action. And for cross-functional orchestration, to ensure speed does not dilute or fragment meaning and vision.

## *Conductor Capabilities*

We have already introduced the four *Conductor Capabilities* that enable leaders to perform at speed and coordinate at scale. This chapter focuses on the two that sit at the heart of strategic decision-making:

### The Two Foundational Conductor Capabilities

Capabilities that set direction and enable coherent action

| Judgement Under Ambiguity | Enterprise Orchestration |
|---|---|
| The ability to make confident, values-led decisions when clarity is partial and speed is high. | The discipline of ensuring decisions travel cleanly across functions without losing context, meaning, or intent. |
| AI accelerates analysis, but only leaders can decide when to pause for reflection and when to move with conviction. | AI speeds up insight, but organisations still struggle to align at the same pace. |
| WHY IT MATTERS | WHY IT MATTERS |
| **It sets the strategic tempo,** ensuring decisions remain coherent even under time pressure. | **It keeps teams moving in rhythm** so execution is coordinated, credible, and sustained under pressure. |
| **Enables clear strategic direction that remains coherent, even when speed and complexity increase.** | **Enables coordinated action where teams operate in rhythm, preserving intent and context from decision through to delivery.** |

**JUDGEMENT SETS THE TEMPO. ORCHESTRATION CARRIES IT ACROSS THE ENTERPRISE.**

Together, they form the foundation of your strategic operating system, the bridge between insight and execution, speed and coherence.

In Chapter 9, we will complete this system by exploring *Adaptive Learning* and *Trust Stewardship*, which sustain rhythm over time.

To understand why these capabilities matter, we must first consider what they replace, and why trust has always been the quiet, invisible barrier between data and decisive action.

## The Pre-AI Baseline

In recent years, data availability has rarely been the critical problem. The challenge has been knowing what data to trust. Even today, with vast data lakes promising to unify truth, they often amplify the same old problem: different truths flowing from the same source.

Analysis paralysis becomes the norm, with endless meetings and repeated requests for 'just one more data-cut'. Decisions get deferred quarter after quarter and the common diagnosis is poor leadership or organisational bureaucracy.

But in my experience, leaders have always instinctively known their inputs were flawed. Information has always been curated not for truth, but to protect the messenger's perspective. Each function optimised its narrative: sales for optimism, operations for capacity, finance for constraint. Leaders received competing truths, all accurate, yet collectively misleading.

Alessandro Ventura, Unilever's VP Technology & Transformation, has lived this shift. Throughout his career, he has rarely seen C-suite decisions benefit from clear-cut information sets and warns that most delays stem not from data scarcity but from rational distrust of curated inputs:

"*Decision quality is only as good as the input you receive. Leaders surround themselves with people they trust, but each has their own bias, so vetted and carefully curated information is presented.*"

Bias is unavoidable. Every perspective carries assumptions, whether human or algorithmic. Leaders have therefore always needed a healthy scepticism toward the information they receive; filtering, contextualising, and ultimately taking responsibility for the final judgement, knowing that this process introduces its own bias as well.

Before AI, the decision trap lay in the sheer effort required to compile volumes of data that could never be fully trusted, followed by high-stakes commitments made on the least shaky foundation possible. Leaders compensated through experience, pattern recognition, insights, and by relying on sources whose past recommendations had proven reliable. This took time, slowed decision-making, and concentrated authority in those with the longest tenure.

AI promised to solve this by delivering objective analysis at scale. Instead, it introduced a new risk. Rather than drowning in subjectively curated data, leaders now risk drowning in confident AI recommendations whose provenance cannot easily be inspected or verified.

Strategic decisions must still be made under uncertainty, but now, they are made faster and with less visible reasoning.

The test of leadership is therefore to exercise judgement when truth feels uncertain. To keep judgement intact whilst moving at speed and knowing when to reconnect so that purpose leads, and when to accelerate so that learning compounds.

This is where individual discipline becomes enterprise rhythm.

## Judgement Under Ambiguity: Reconnecting Before Executing

Pre-AI, leaders doubted the inputs. Now, you must doubt the outputs. AI delivers confident answers without always revealing how they were formed, so the task is to exercise sound judgement with only partial clarity, especially when certainty itself may mislead.

The *Guidance Centre* anchors intention and serves the enterprise. It builds capability and trust, and when the two stay connected, speed becomes purposeful rather than reactive. Here, you scale that pattern under time pressure.

Judgement Under Ambiguity is the discipline of making confident, values-aligned decisions when clarity is partial and certainty is misleading. It's the ability to act decisively without needing absolute clarity. In practice, this means knowing when to pause for reconnection and when to accelerate for learning. You link your own centres of logic, purpose, and instinct to the organisation's shared lenses, and the four voices of the AI Board Consult can help you with this part.

Alessandro presents this well: "*AI can be incredibly helpful doing the groundwork and providing objectivity, especially at an operational level. But the process and quality of decision-making still rest with our critical human judgement. We are a long way off AI making strategic decisions itself.*"

The repeatable rhythm is simple: Reconnect → Reframe → Run (learn) → Review.

Guidance, courage, and execution to give speed without losing judgement.

Even so, overreliance on AI risks undermining critical skills. Alessandro warns of the long-term risk, "*The erosion of critical skills through blind reliance is real; we stop training those leadership muscles. Imagine a CFO who hasn't managed the ledger, a marketer who hasn't run consumer panels, both now just managing AI-driven dashboards. The risk is enormous.*"

Every time urgency tempts you to act because 'AI quickly gives the answer', pause. That pause protects coherence. Judgement under ambiguity ensures speed serves wisdom, not the reverse.

The next step is application with structure, a repeatable rhythm that turns reflection into action without losing integrity.

## Putting Judgement Under Ambiguity Into Practice

Good decision-making in the AI era goes beyond just knowing *what* to do, to clarify *why* you're doing it and *what* outcome you want to achieve. When speed increases and data multiplies, judgement doesn't disappear; it must become sharper, more explicit, and more visible.

AI excels at detection and speed but struggles with context, ethics, and ambiguity. Leaders compensate by applying three repeatable steps:

1. **Frame the Question**

   **Why:** If you ask the wrong question, AI will optimise the wrong problem or your bias.
   **How:** Reconnect to guidance; what decision are we really making? What serves the enterprise, not just my function?
   **Outcome:** *Clarity of purpose.* Analysis aligns with the true strategic stake.

2. **Interpret the Results**

   **Why:** AI finds patterns; humans assign meaning.
   **How:** Test which results still hold if conditions shift? What did the model miss: people, ethics, timing?
   **Outcome:** *Anchored insight.* You move from output to informed choice.

3. **Override with Intent**

   **Why:** Automated confidence seduces leaders into silence.
   **How:** If you go against AI's logic, document why. Treat it as organisational learning.
   **Outcome:** *Balanced integration of data and judgement.* Each override strengthens future wisdom.

**In summary:**

Judgement Under Ambiguity ensures that speed serves wisdom, not the reverse. When these three steps become habit, decisions are faster and safer, grounded in purpose, validated by reasoning, and resilient under scrutiny.

## Enterprise Orchestration: Making Decisions Travel

Judgement Under Ambiguity sets the music tempo, and Enterprise Orchestration ensures that music travels. It's the discipline of designing for decisions to move across functions without losing coherence. It turns isolated excellence into enterprise value.

AI has compressed analysis times, but coordination still lags. When insights move faster than alignment, impact is lost long before execution. Orchestration closes that gap by establishing shared language, roles, and rhythms that let ideas flow from origin to outcome.

As Alessandro notes, *"Traditional functional silos no longer match how work gets done, which is why we see the industry trend moving toward process-based rather than function-based organisations."*

As a result, Unilever is creating a single organisation, Customer Operations, to serve its customers best. This organisation merges parts of four different functions into one. It's a practical example of the shift from functional optimisation to cross-functional orchestration, and decisions can travel because they have one structure, one rhythm, and one shared purpose.

At ABB Electrification, Massimo echoes the same principle, *"In my strategy role, I interact with all functions, and I always ensure we have at least the finance, strategy, and HR functions on the same page, to work in an integrated manner with other functions where required."*

ABB's transformation of the customer journey includes mapping ten process steps and exploring AI agents to simplify and synchronise them because functional siloes can't keep pace. "*Coordination isn't the only difficulty with a project like this, but maintaining coherence as decisions travel. We always look at the integrated impact, not just what strategy delivers, but how it affects the entire value chain. Orchestration only works when every function sees its reflection in the same outcome.*"

That's orchestration at scale, where decisions travel with context intact, clear ownership, and sustained rhythm. When structure catches up with flow, coherence scales from individuals to enterprises.

Massimo summarises it well, "*Our goal is to make decisions travel with the same clarity they were made with. When every team understands both the reasoning and the rhythm, alignment becomes self-sustaining.*"

When decision flow meets organisational friction, orchestration reaches its limit, and structure must evolve. That evolution begins in Chapter 7.

## The Strategic Close: Making Decisions into Momentum

Even with orchestration in place, decisions can still fragment unless they are captured with discipline. The *Strategic Close* ensures every major decision leaves the room ready to travel, clear, complete, and owned.

The principle is to express every major decision on one page. It captures what was decided, why it matters, what was traded, and how success will be measured. Compression forces clarity, and clarity accelerates action.

Alessandro describes this discipline, *"We document the logic clearly, so everyone understands not just what we decided but why, and what we're watching for. That clarity enables execution."*

This clarity travels fast because each function understands its relevant implications, and the story holds coherence even as different functions interpret it through their realities.

The Strategic Close ensures continuity in rhythm across the enterprise. As that rhythm strengthens, structure becomes the next constraint, and we will explore this in the next chapter.

## Guardrails: Protecting Judgement at Speed

Alessandro warns against 'messianic expectations' of AI. Use it to refine thinking, not replace it. Like my experience in Paris, we have all experienced untrustworthy AI recommendations, so we can benefit from its power, but define clear limits.

The risk intensifies with AI agents. When one agent's small error becomes another's input, flaws compound invisibly until the recommendations themselves drift off course. As Alessandro puts it, *"Agents may and will drift; they start producing accurate outputs and recommendations, but when they become marginally less accurate, the potential scale of damage can be significant."*

Guardrails are needed to preserve AI's value whilst protecting guidance-connected judgement:

- **Explainability:** If an AI recommendation can't be explained, don't scale it.
- **Human-in-Loop:** Require human sign-off for irreversible decisions. Guidance validates before Action executes.
- **Bias Checks:** Review training data and outcome equity quarterly to prevent automating historical bias.
- **Kill-Switch:** Name accountable owners and rollback plans for high-risk deployments.
- **Transparency:** Make AI performance, fairness measures, and trade-offs visible. Trust grows through visibility.

These disciplines offer a structure that stops speed from destroying trust. With guardrails in place, acceleration becomes sustainable, and flow remains guided.

## The Human Core: Where Flow Begins

Alessandro reminds us that AI transformations ultimately rise or fall on trust and advises that we must *"learn to use the machine effectively, but never think like a machine. Retain human critical thinking and foster relationships and collaborative thinking."*

Judgement sets the rhythm, and orchestration ensures that the rhythm travels. Trust helps keep the rhythm steady when pressure mounts, but because trust doesn't travel automatically through proximity or hierarchy, it must be deliberately stewarded. Trust Stewardship is the third conductor capability, and in Chapter 9, we see how it helps sustain confidence and clarity at scale.

## Practical Application:

Apply these capabilities to one strategic decision this week:

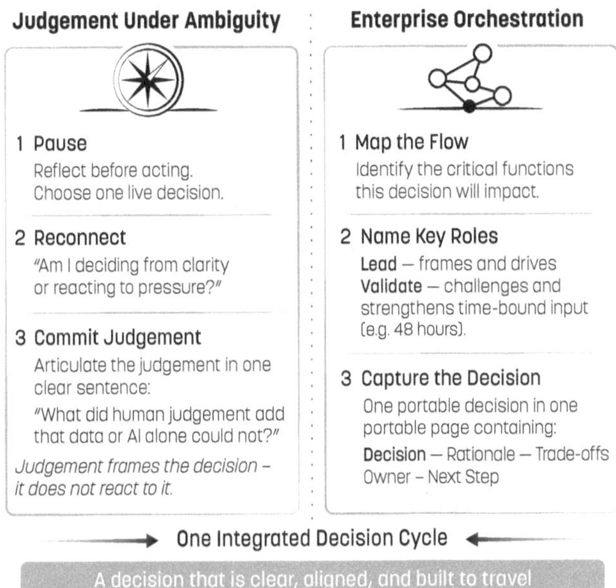


*Watch how clarity changes the conversation. That's judgement and orchestration working together, speed guided by trust, coherence in motion.*

**Ritual:** Weekly Reconnection Check (15 minutes). Before one strategic decision each week, pause and document: 'Am I operating from Guidance Centre or disconnected Action Centre?'

**Metric:** *Decision Velocity* × *First-Time-Right Percentage.* Track decisions made faster AND requiring less rework. Target: 20% improvement within ninety days.

**If You Remember One Thing:** AI accelerates analysis and action, but only you decide what drives that speed. Judgement Under Ambiguity keeps leaders decisive when clarity is partial; Enterprise Orchestration ensures those decisions travel coherently.

**Where This Takes You Next:** Building on your strategic decision-making and *Conductor Capabilities*, as we move into the *Amplify* stage, where leadership shifts from individual judgement to organisational design.

# PART III

# Amplify team capability

## (Leading Others)

*Turn team anxiety into shared ownership and capability. Develop Conductors who can coordinate across boundaries whilst preserving deep expertise. When leaders model open reasoning and genuine AI partnership, trust deepens, learning accelerates, and distributed judgement scales without losing alignment.*

CHAPTER 7

# WHEN STRUCTURE BECOMES A BOTTLENECK

# Building organisations that move at AI speed

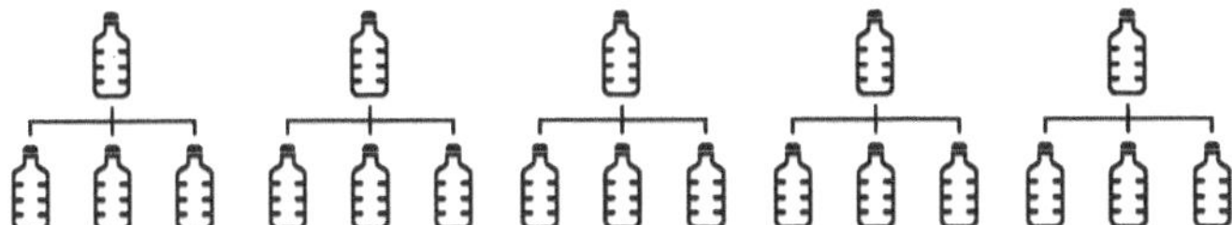

*"Do we have all the capabilities needed to launch our new service lines in new markets, whilst also improving service quality?"*

This simple question posed last year by a CEO to Antony Shields, now Global People Operations Director at Baker McKenzie, exposed why traditional structures break under AI speed.

Antony explained, *"The request sounds straightforward until you attempt to answer it accurately. I need to know our internal skills and capabilities, gaps for external expertise, who can move internally, and who can be reskilled at speed — all while maintaining quality."*

Traditional workforce modelling and rigid structures can't answer these questions. Data sits in silos, learning is disconnected from recruitment, performance is split from capability inventories, and strategy is invisible to development planning. Each function optimises in isolation, but together, they create fragmentation, and no one can synthesise all this simultaneously.

*"The crisis at a micro level,"* Antony explains, *"is telling employees that 'their career is theirs to build,' but then tolerating platforms and tools that limit the realisation of this due to data being siloed. When companies are set up in functional silos, and yet careers, capability development, and mobility cut across them, it begins to limit performance. The ability to offer even meaningful automated and dynamic career plans is virtually zero."*

When micro failures scale to macro pressures, a crisis becomes likely. There's no doubt that organisational complexity requires structure and order, but when these get in the way of business requirements and value delivery, the balance needs to change. We have all witnessed Matrix, Team-based, Networked, Lean, and more recently, Agile and Teal organisation structures, but whilst each has merit, none has been comprehensively successful. Leaders are still facing questions that their structures cannot answer.

This chapter focuses on the leadership behaviours that make structural and operational change possible. Without them, even the best operating model will falter.

We already understand the importance of your conductor identity and its role to orchestrate rather than execute. But conducting across siloed functions is nearly impossible when accountability fragments among executives optimising for different outcomes. Judgement may be sound, and intent may be strong, yet decisions still stall at functional boundaries.

Convergence is the structural condition in which work, decisions, and accountability align across functions, allowing orchestration to become possible. Without it, even the best judgement and intent stalls within organisational boundaries.

When your CEO asks questions that your structure cannot even model, answers need to be forced across fragmented systems. Functional boundaries block the flow of work, distort accountability, and make it impossible to respond to enterprise-level performance questions. Convergence is no longer optional; it's the condition to make modern leadership viable.

## Why AI-Enabled Convergence Succeeds Where Matrix and Agile Fell Short

From the 1970s onward, organisations attempted to solve functional boundary problems through a wide and varied range of organisational structures. But these all added coordination layers without changing how decisions moved or resources flowed. Matrix created dual reporting whilst keeping power in silos. Agile renamed teams but preserved boundaries.

AI changes the equation. Instead of adding layers, it enables real-time intelligence flows that let decision rights and resources move dynamically toward outcomes. Structure becomes a bottleneck when the timings of strategic priorities, operational demands, and human coordination fall out of sync.

The trap is restructuring before building capability. Without coordination discipline, accountability concentrates on leaders who cannot yet integrate effectively. Antony's success reversed this sequence: capability first, structure second. Convergence followed readiness, not reorganisation.

## The Three-Part Future: Where Convergence Takes Us

Answering questions like the one posed by a CEO to Antony requires dismantling silos and creating a three-part model for convergence. This model enables what researchers call ambidexterity, the ability to explore new opportunities whilst exploiting existing capabilities simultaneously.

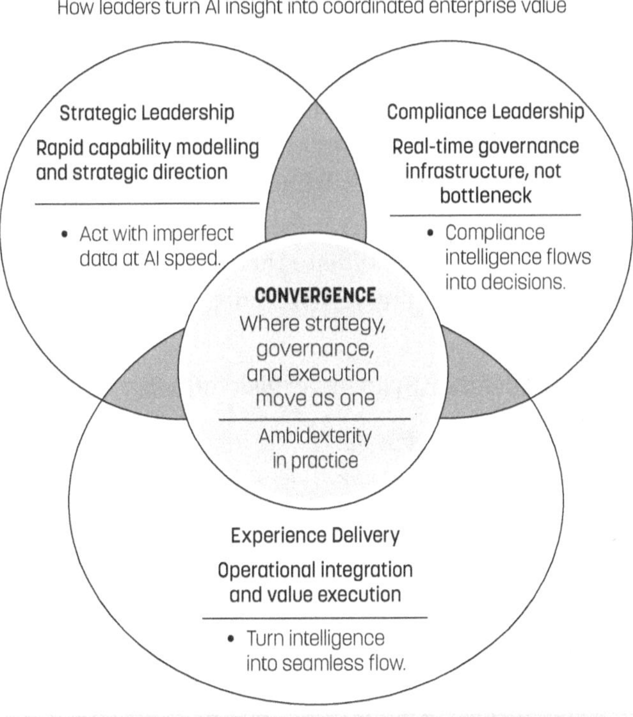


Convergence turns functional leaders into enterprise orchestrators.

### 1. Strategic Leadership: Rapid Capability Modelling

*"For the first time, the CHRO with AI can quickly model what growth delivery looks like from a people perspective."* Antony goes on to add: *"We can help the CEO understand his growth requirements without spending years with consultants on partially accurate workforce planning."*

But modelling isn't delivering. AI can indicate a need for specific capabilities across new markets within months. It can calculate optimal build-versus-buy ratios. It can project quality impact from rapid scaling. What it cannot do is coordinate Learning's development timelines with Talent's recruitment cycles, Finance's budget releases and Operations' quality standards. All of these move simultaneously rather than sequentially.

This prioritises business outcomes first, capability requirements second, and organisational solutions third. Operating at speed with imperfect data rather than waiting for analytical precision. This is an exploration capability where you scan opportunities, model possibilities, and enable strategic agility.

Many organisations fail here by building skills taxonomies bottom-up without connecting to strategic priorities. They catalogue capabilities whilst missing what matters: which business outcomes need these capabilities, and how quickly must we deploy them? AI-powered insights don't automatically create coordinated action; you can have perfect visibility, whilst functional boundaries prevent acting at competitive speed.

### 2. Compliance Leadership: Systematic Risk Infrastructure

*"The compliance piece is absolutely set for AI,"* Antony notes. *"You need guardrails to safeguard what you're doing as well as the data, however, AI can handle the heavy multi-jurisdictional complexity that humans struggle with."*

Compliance becomes infrastructure rather than function, operating systematically across all processes rather than sitting separately. This is governance enabling both exploration and exploitation without creating chaos or risk. AI automates compliance checking, but convergence ensures that compliance intelligence informs strategic and operational decisions in real time rather than retrospectively through functional review cycles.

### 3. Experience Delivery: Operational Integration

*"I think our understanding of HR now across the hire-to-retire cycle will become more of an operations role," says* Antony. *"How do you operationally drive value? How do you create experiences both internally and externally that enable that value creation? That's where AI has a huge role because the functions have already done the hard work to get the data there — it's just not being used effectively."*

This platform approach mirrors how technology companies organise around platforms rather than products. They execute efficiently, scale what works, and deliver consistent value whilst enabling local adaptation. But here's the convergence imperative: AI can access data across functions, but only converged structures enable coordinated action on that intelligence. Strategic modelling shows what's needed. Compliance frameworks show what's permissible. Experience delivery must execute both simultaneously, and that demands organisational flows, not functional handoffs.

## Goal-Based Validation at Scale

Hemerson Paes, Senior Global Network Catalyst at Roche, demonstrates the three-part model discussed above and at scale. Roche has over 4,000 people connected to a goal-based marketplace, proving chance serves to enables strategic delivery when built systematically.

*"An example goal might be to reduce breast cancer in a particular Southeast Asia population,"* Hemerson explains. *"There is a distinct project based on that goal, and interested people can sign up to support this ambition. We have avoided scrum or agile squads; this is a goal-oriented team that becomes self-managing."*

Effective convergence organises around outcomes, not structures. Roche doesn't ask '*What skills do you have?*' but '*What goals actually matter?*' Teams form, accomplish objectives, dissolve, and reform around new priorities.

As Hemerson said, this isn't agile repackaged because those efforts renamed teams without changing how decisions were made. Roche has created several unique differences: systematic capability, strategic clarity about goals, compliance infrastructure that travels with fluid teams, operational platforms that enable marketplace mechanics, and goal-based teams that are operationally viable.

Network analysis reveals 70 to 80% of work happens within teams invisible to traditional organisational structures. Line managers have limited knowledge of what employees actually do, because work flows through project-based collaboration rather than hierarchical assignment.

Hemerson's data shows people are four times more likely to join goal-based teams than to apply for traditional role rotations. When you organise around meaningful objectives rather than functional assignments, engagement increases because purpose becomes visible.

The Roche example illustrates that outcome-focused convergence is already happening. The concept of convergence should no longer be the question, but whether you can do it systematically before speed turns your structure into a liability.

## What Makes Convergence Work: AI-Coordination Without Bureaucracy

Convergence requires coordination systems that work across functions at enterprise-decision speed. Your mechanism might be cross-functional decision protocols from Chapters 5 and 6, goal-based team structures like at Roche, or AI-enabled decision infrastructure that integrates insight, escalation, and governance in real time.

The principle is that strategic questions that span functions require coordination to replace slow, sequential consultation with real-time integration.

AI creates a genuine middle ground beyond centralisation debates. Local leaders get autonomy in adapting to their context, whilst central functions maintain visibility and intervene when patterns indicate problems. You don't choose between consistency and adaptation. AI enables local autonomy within systematic guardrails, ensuring alignment with strategic priorities.

For convergence, this means flattening hierarchies without creating chaos. Local teams assemble capabilities around goals, make decisions suiting their context, and operate at speed. Central coordination ensures strategic alignment through systematic intelligence rather than approval hierarchies.

## Conductor Capability at Scale

Convergence extends the conductor mindset beyond coordination into design; it's no longer about managing across boundaries but removing them entirely. *Show–Solo–Share* is the decision discipline that now scales this mindset and helps leaders model outcome-focused thinking to practice on goal-based challenges.

This shift from hero to conductor becomes essential. You cannot orchestrate capability flows whilst defending functional boundaries. You cannot enable goal-oriented teams whilst maintaining hierarchical control. You cannot deliver integrated experiences whilst optimising isolated departmental metrics.

## Transformation Measurement

Convergence requires measurement systems to evolve alongside structural change. Traditional functional metrics — such as time to hire, training hours, or departmental budgets — optimise for silo efficiency and make integrated performance invisible.

Converged metrics, by contrast, focus on speed to outcome, goal-based contribution, and strategic agility. They are harder to measure, but far more valuable at the enterprise level.

Converged organisations track outcome delivery speed: how many days pass from strategic question to capability deployed?

Goal-based contribution: did teams achieve measurable impact?

Strategic response capability: how quickly does capability flow to new priorities?

Ambidexterity effectiveness: can the organisation explore new opportunities while exploiting existing capabilities?

What organisations choose to measure signals what they value. Functional metrics reinforce functional behaviour. Outcome-based metrics make integrated performance visible — and therefore possible.

## The Identity and Power Shift: Why Convergence Feels Hard

Convergence can threaten power structures because of redistributed authority. Functional heads lose budget control, headcount, and approval authority. Operational resistance is inevitable and legitimate, because it's an identity transformation as already addressed. Leaders who built careers on owning departments must now lead without walls and become conductors of fluid teams and distributed decisions.

Some leaders embrace this evolution, recognising that AI-powered convergence creates better outcomes. Others resist because the identity shift feels like a capability loss.

Clinging to functional authority feels safe, but it's a temporary illusion. The choice shouldn't be comfort vs change, but a deliberate evolution to avoid forced irrelevance.

Converged organisations outpace functionally structured competitors. I therefore believe we're not fighting between comfort and change, but between deliberate evolution and forced irrelevance.

Antony chose evolution. Six months after implementing the convergence architecture, the results validate that choice. Leadership receives growth capability answers in weeks, not years. Hemerson's teams show four times higher engagement than traditional structures whilst delivering measurable impact on strategic priorities. Both prove convergence is an operational architecture enabling AI-era performance.

## Connecting to Strategic Decision-Making

The Strengthen and Partner stages helped build the disciplines of judgement and orchestration, and tools to make decisions that are sound, transparent, and shared. But capability alone is not enough. When those decisions meet legacy structures, coordination slows, ownership fragments, and execution falters.

In the Amplify stage now, convergence provides the missing architecture and turns the rhythm of decision-making into behaviours where intelligence can move at the same speed as intent. Instead of passing through sequential approvals or departmental gates, insight, accountability, and resources converge around the outcomes that matter most.

In converged systems, the AI Board Consult becomes an operating mechanism, not a workshop. Its systematic challenge feeds directly into goal-based teams that can act immediately, without waiting for functional alignment. Strategic compression travels faster because structural friction has been designed out.

This is the shift from *decision flow* to *organisational flow*, from leaders coordinating decisions to organisations built to move with them. Convergence doesn't replace good decision-making; it multiplies its impact.

## Your First Convergence Experiment

Apply convergence to one strategic priority rather than attempting wholesale transformation. Choose a board-level objective where functional boundaries create friction. Design one cross-functional cell with real decision authority, clear outcome metrics, and systematic infrastructure support.

Run for thirty days, extract learning, and share systematically using Show-Solo-Share to build distributed convergence capability.

When a CEO asked Antony, "*How do we launch new service lines whilst improving quality?*" traditional HR couldn't answer. With AI enablement and a convergence architecture, that same question can now answered in days, with clear capability deployment timelines, investment requirements, and risk mitigation plans. The Board and senior leadership can leverage disparate people data and AI to support growth decisions with confidence. Strategic opportunities don't wait for functional coordination to catch up.

That's what convergence enables. Not just faster coordination, but structural capacity to act on strategic intelligence at the speed competitive conditions demand.

Convergence is no longer optional in the AI era. It's now your choice as to whether you lead it deliberately, building *Conductor Capabilities*, or wait until competitor pressure forces you to make the changes.

### Ritual: Monthly Convergence Review

Each month, pick one strategic objective and ask: Did convergence accelerate delivery, or did functional boundaries slow us down? Document the patterns and see where goal-based teams outpaced silos, see what systematic intelligence enabled integration, and which *Conductor Capabilities* mattered most.

Share your insights with other leadership teams to compound organisational learning about convergence in practice.

### Metric: *Strategic Response Time*

Track strategic response times, i.e. number of days from question to committed action. Target: 50% faster through integrated operations vs sequential planning. Add secondary metrics: goal-based engagement, informal network activity, capability deployment speed, and ambidexterity balance.

## The Leadership Challenge Convergence Creates

Research shows that up to 80% of work happens in teams invisible to traditional organisational structures. Work therefore flows through trust and expertise, and hierarchy is simply how we pay and manage people.

AI accelerates this shift toward team-based work by enabling functional convergence and fluid team formation. Leadership can no longer operate through rigid hierarchical structures when most of the work happens outside them.

Line managers have limited visibility on the exact day-to-day tasks an employee handles, because work moves through project-based collaboration rather than hierarchical assignment. Traditional performance management, resource allocation, and capability development all assume stable reporting lines, but convergence dissolves those assumptions.

Your leadership role during this evolution is to enable fluidity without losing coherence. When 80% of work travels through invisible teams, the old structures like hierarchy, performance reviews, and resource allocation all fall short.

The real challenge is working out how to build capability when the flow of work is now starting to ignore historical org charts. Chapter 8 answers this.

**If You Remember One Thing:** Convergence is the structural shift aligning accountability with outcomes that AI makes urgent. It moves decision rights and resources to outcome-focused teams, replacing hierarchy with systematic intelligence.

**Where This Takes You Next:** You've reshaped organisational flows around strategic outcomes. When work becomes fluid and invisible to traditional structures, the challenge becomes how to develop capability when teams form, deliver, dissolve, and reform. Next, we introduce systemic learning — how capability must flow at the same pace as work.

CHAPTER 8

# SYSTEMIC LEARNING CAPABILITY FOR AI-ERA LEADERSHIP

# *Trained yet unprepared*

In 2008, my company delivered Lehman Brothers' global mandatory training. Every trader and desk head had completed their training certifications and extensive mandatory risk-management programmes. Green ticks all round....

Yet, months later, I stood on the 31st floor in their London office in disbelief as a 158-year-old institution collapsed.

That moment shaped me. Building compliance is not the same as building capability.

*Procedures without judgement become training without learning.*

Enforced training provides a measure of knowledge and healthy completion metrics, but it doesn't change beliefs, behaviours, and the way critical decisions are made under pressure, or when conflicting incentives collide. With this approach to training, capability and judgement are unmeasured and therefore undeveloped.

When organisations fail, it's rarely because people lack information; it's because they haven't developed the judgement to apply that information under pressure.

The Lehman Brothers' employees in question were equipped with knowledge, not judgement.

That experience reinforced in me the importance of creating a learning culture that embeds systemic attitudes guiding behaviours and judgement and provides the capabilities that actually determine outcomes and ultimately enterprise value.

Years later, the same underlying tensions exist in most organisations: measuring learning and the gap to enabling people to apply judgement in real work.

Simon Brown, the Chief Learning Officer at a Big Four Professional Services Firm explains, "*To date, 350,000 employees have completed a general awareness AI learning and over 100,000 in-depth AI badges. The stats are impressive, but we still see challenges with teams struggling to apply AI in ways that improve outcomes. There is still lots to do to prepare people for this new era reality of AI.*"

The tension is not effort versus neglect, but learning metrics versus applied judgement. Even when learning has scaled, the challenge is ensuring it shows up in decisions, behaviours, and results. This challenge becomes particularly urgent in the AI era. The traditional approach to learning assumed space to learn before implementing, so organisations could design, roll out, and measure adoption. AI erases the gap between learning and applying. Change is now simultaneous and continuous for every function. When AI capability doubles every few months, the gap between training cycles and capability requirements doesn't narrow, but compounds exponentially.

You cannot train your way into readiness when capability needs evolve faster than programmes can be delivered. Companies rarely fail from a lack of knowledge. They fail when judgement collapses under pressure. As AI compounds exponentially, pressure is increasing, so the goal for learning must therefore be to enhance judgement and start tracking readiness. Systemic Learning in the flow of work becomes your solution.

Yet recognising the need is one thing, rebuilding the system is another. Turning an established organisation is like turning an oil tanker — slow, deliberate, requiring sustained force. Simon understands how difficult this task is: "W*e need to get better at measuring whether people can actually build and apply new skills to solve new problems faster than problems evolve?*"

Simon is clear that organisations need top-down support and commitment. "*Leadership must support AI-related learning, for that learning to be embedded in how we think and interact with our work. Boards must prioritise this as vigorously as strategy and finance. Without that top-down commitment, learning becomes something people do around work rather than through it.*"

This is not a training gap, but, in my view, an architectural failure. Fixing it means reimagining learning as a system embedded in work, rather than a parallel activity.

## Today's Learning Model Fails, But AI Makes It Worse

Charles Jennings, the former CLO at Reuters, explains why most organisations struggle: *"Organisations fail because they're asking the wrong questions such as, 'What skills do people need?' when they should actually ask, 'What performance must we achieve and what capabilities enable that performance?' Those are fundamentally different questions leading to completely different architectures."*

This approach was possible when work was more stable and predictable, but AI now changes everything. The flaw with the traditional approach is the gap between *learning activity* and *hope* that new skills transfer into better business outcomes.

**Traditional learning asks:** 'What skills do people need?'
It starts with job roles, then competencies, then skills, then training, and then the hope that this will transfer to work.

Conversely, Systemic Learning first analyses the business objectives and aligns learning within work activities:

**Systemic Learning asks:** 'What performance must we achieve, and what capabilities enable it?'

It starts with results, then critical tasks, then capabilities, and finally solutions embedded in work. The difference is unmistakable:

**Traditional Learning**

Linear. Detached. Sequential.

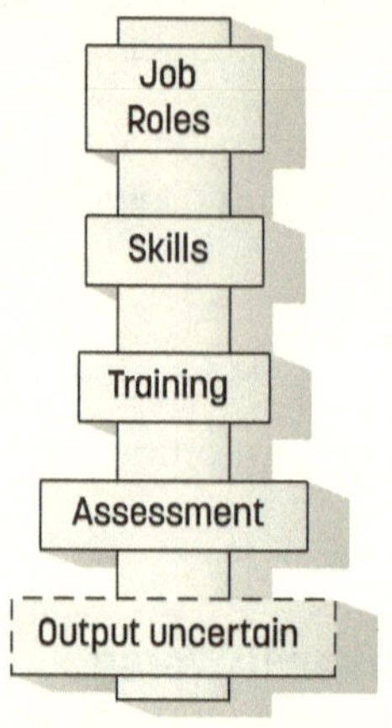


Traditional learning starts with skills and hopes they transfer into results.

It operates in silos, develops people sequentially, and lags behind real work.

**What skills do people need?**

**Systemic Learning**

Integrated. Outcome-Driven. Embedded.

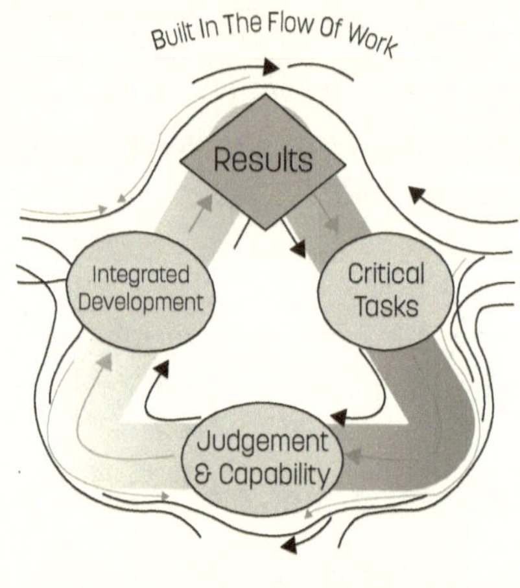


Systemic Learning embeds capability into work, turning training into distributed intelligence.

**What performance must we achieve, and what capabilities enable it?**

The gap between these approaches determines whether AI investment builds capability or merely fills your LMS with green ticks. Remember your sparring-partnership practice from Chapter 2? You didn't learn AI collaboration through a prompt-engineering course; you developed it by practising with real tasks and applying systematic challenge to your thinking on real decisions.

This same principle applies to the convergence challenge from Chapter 7. When you flatten hierarchies and merge functions, you create cross-boundary dependencies requiring simultaneous coordination across multiple teams. Traditional learning can't build this capability because it develops skills sequentially, normally within one isolated function. By the time everyone is trained, the dependencies have already shifted.

Systemic Learning solves this by building capability at the point of coordination, in the flow of cross-functional work itself.

**Learning Debt:** When Speed Outpaces Adaptation

Few organisations track what I call learning debt, the capability erosion that accumulates when work accelerates faster than people can develop the judgement to sustain it. Pre-AI, when operating environments were slower, this debt rarely needed to be measured, because experience accumulated through repetition and feedback loops, and the gaps in judgement surfaced gradually. AI, however, changes this dynamic.

Learning debt compounds silently across every level. Junior analysts automate basic work without developing the pattern recognition that makes analysis valuable. Mid-level managers delegate coordination to AI without building the orchestration judgement that makes executives effective. Each automation creates immediate productivity but incurs future capability cost, visible only when complexity increases and automation breaks.

When AI automates foundational tasks, it erases the practice that builds judgement, regardless of whether in law, engineering, or finance.

The implication is profound, and Simon sees this accelerating, *"Regardless of which statistics you believe, certain roles will become redundant, but many new ones will emerge with higher-value work. The question is whether people will have consistently developed the judgement they need to evolve at the right pace."*

Charles illustrates this through a medical example, *"Consider a doctor becomes an expert through years of graft, building pattern recognition that makes them great diagnosticians. If AI handles all basic diagnostics, where does that expertise pathway come from?"*

The tasks AI automates aren't just simple processes; they're the development pathway that builds expertise. Remove learning opportunities without replacement, and capabilities will erode slowly and invisibly. Eventually, judgement will no longer exist.

This is why I recommend that every automation decision ask two questions:

1. What human capability did this task traditionally develop?
2. How will we replace that development experience?

A legitimate provocation is that as AI continues to improve, declining human capability may not matter. There is some truth in this. But it's a dangerous narrative as it shifts responsibility away from leadership and treats judgement as something that can be rented on demand rather than cultivated, rehearsed, and renewed. Organisations that stop stretching human capability rarely notice the damage until complexity spikes and AI can no longer arbitrate trade-offs, values, or unintended consequences.

Without addressing both the above questions, organisations trade short-term productivity for long-term capability bankruptcy. Learning debt silently erases expertise, and often proves more damaging than knowledge gaps, because it goes unmeasured until complexity demands judgement that no longer exists.

## The Learning Rate Formula: A Predictor of Success

A former Intel executive shared a deceptively simple insight that remains profoundly relevant:

*'If the rate of organisational learning matches or exceeds the rate of change, business success is likely. If it falls behind, business failure is probable.'*

As AI accelerates the rate of change, organisations that aspire to improve performance must work harder than ever to ensure their rate of learning matches and ideally exceeds this rate of change.

This elevates the importance of learning from an HR activity into a leadership and business KPI. Learning rate connects to the Amplify stage of SPAR, measured through:

**Learning Rate:** How quickly do teams move from exposure to autonomous performance on priority tasks or flows? Aim to measure whether capability is compounding faster than change, and therefore, competitive readiness.

**Decision Quality and Throughput:** Are strategic decisions being made faster and with fewer reversals? Track decision lead time (from problem to committed action) and first-time-right rate (decisions not needing rework). Validate that learning is actually improving judgement whilst under pressure.

**Strategy-to-Value Lead Time:** It's important to measure how long it takes for a decision to translate into measurable enterprise value. With this in mind, learning is then seen as a success determinant, but it raises a question. '*How do you build learning capability that compounds as fast as change itself?*'

Partially because of legacy platforms and HR heritage, L&D typically designs learning solutions bottom-up, individual by individual. The issue with this is it is disconnected from how teams actually work or how they need to be able to adapt as organisational needs evolve. Simon is acutely aware of this gap, "*Individual awareness means nothing without organisational capability. We need top-down architecture and bottom-up energy meeting in the middle.*"

When learning sits below strategy rather than inside it, effort without readiness is the primary by-product. Traditional metrics measure attendance or short-term knowledge retention, whilst the real prize is organisational learning rate, the rate at which the entire system develops judgement and adapts to new conditions. Capability debt then accumulates, and the organisation learns more slowly than its environment evolves.

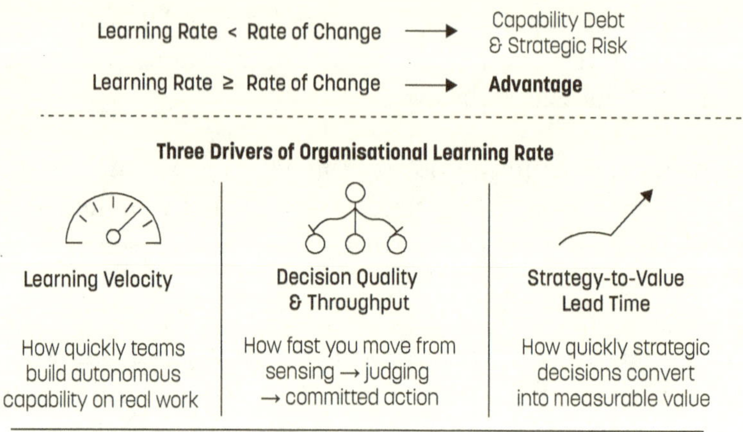


The Learning Rate formula gives you the diagnostic, and Systemic Learning provides the structure to solve it.

## Systemic Learning at Scale

The goal is to embed capability into the flow of work and put skill-building into the central operating system. It must become a living system where insights travel quickly, pathways strengthen through repeated use, and the whole network becomes smarter with every cycle. In practice, this means creating a system where:

- A **'Neural Core'** (central L&D/strategy) sets standards, provides governance, and circulates proven patterns and insights.
- **'Local Neurons'** (teams and functions) adapt these insights to their real-world challenges and feed their successes and failures back into the core.
- **'Learning Pathways'** are the connections that allow successful solutions to spread instantly and failed experiments to be retired quickly.

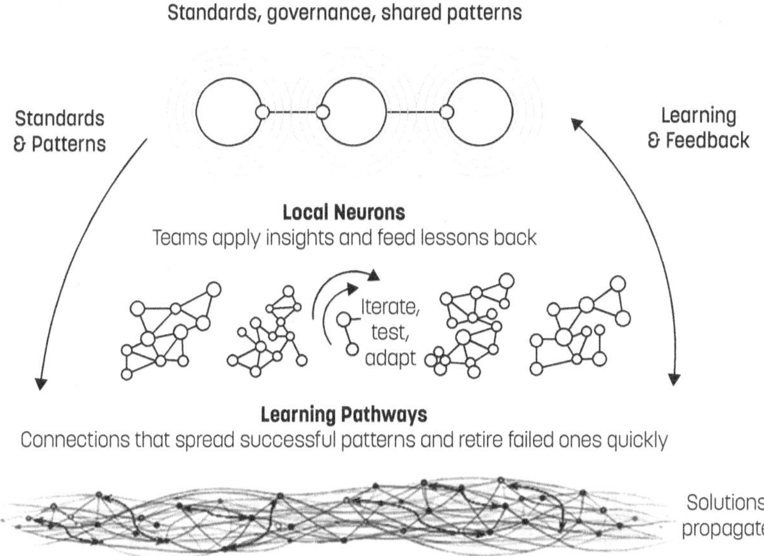


Systemic Learning embeds capability within work.

The Neural Core sets standards, Local Neurons adapt them, and Learning Pathways spread insight at network speed.

Together they form a living system where organisational intelligence compounds faster than change.

This approach pivots L&D from a content distributor into an intelligence circulator, the antithesis of a centralised library, but a living, responsive system for capability distribution where feedback loops (project reviews, decision retrospectives, AI-assisted knowledge capture) act as neural pathways, constantly strengthening organisational judgement.

Neural networks strengthen through self-propagation, constantly adjusting based on feedback. In practice, this means teams share what worked and what failed, feeding those lessons back into the system. The faster that feedback travels, the faster organisational intelligence evolves.

When knowledge moves through the enterprise as quickly as technology advances, learning debt gets eliminated rather than accumulated. When insights compound faster than problems evolve, the organisation maintains a learning rate ahead of its change rate. This is how you turn the Learning Rate Formula from theory into reality.

## Six Principles to Build a Living Learning System

Six principles separate organisations that build living learning systems from those who still rely on 'training'. Together, they create a Neural Network Architecture:

1. **Consider results, not programmes**
   Focus on business results and map critical tasks that drive them. Identify team-level capability gaps, not just individual skill deficits.

2. **Embed support throughout workflow**
   Integrate checklists, exemplars, AI prompts, and quality standards directly into the flow of work. Integration closes the transfer gap between learning and application.

3. **Design for expertise development**
   Use simulations, reflection, and progressive challenge to maintain expertise pathways even as AI handles the basics.

4. **Build through peer networks**
   Encourage systemic peer learning through after-action reviews and reusable patterns that travel across teams. When one team solves a problem, capture not just the solution but the reasoning behind it, making it adaptable for others facing similar challenges.

5. **Measure learning rate**
   Monitor time-to-capability, first-time-right percentages, decision-rework rates, and quality indicators.

6. **Align accountability to outcomes**
   Link capability-development success metrics to enterprise performance.

When these principles operate together, learning transforms from calendar events into a living system that adapts as fast as business realities.

## Making the Architecture Operational

Simon's internal agent marketplace demonstrates this approach at scale. The team built a system where people publish and reuse AI solutions. *"Our agent-builder has clear governance to assess when an agent migrates from personal to shared use. The benefit is compounding reuse, fewer duplicate builds, faster time-to-capability, and quality that improves with every use."*

Teams build solutions for their specific challenges. Successful agents move to the marketplace, and others then adapt them. The neural core provides governance whilst local neurons create contextual applications. Learning compounds across the organisation rather than remaining siloed in functional training programmes.

Like any living system, maintenance is required, and as Simon explains, agents are no different, *"We train agents and then essentially 'performance-manage' them, promote the good ones, and retire the bad ones. In some ways, it's a process similar to managing employees."*

With governance and maintenance taking place within the Neural Network, Systemic Learning can begin to bloom. Within the same firm, they are transitioning to learning in the flow of work wherever possible, and this is nicely illustrated by their 'Future Hacks' programme. Part learning and part hackathon, teams identify AI use cases, build an agent to perform that task, and not only do they solve a business problem, they also learn at the same time.

What differentiates this example from most traditional learning is the combination of peer-to-peer connection and learning experience applied directly to the job. As Charles observes, *"It's focusing on team learning, not just individual learning. Teams are the 'atomic units' of value in today's organisations, and focusing on individual development alone misses a critical opportunity."*

## From Functional Silos to Distributed Intelligence

The traditional L&D model fails because it treats learning as something separate from work. Global Centres of Excellence typically 'push' standardised programmes, whilst functions deliver their own targeted training. Content overlaps, stakeholders compete for attention and budget, and learners follow their duty to 'complete' assigned modules. L&D measures success by completion rates and satisfaction scores, which are fundamentally disconnected from actual job performance. Critical skill gaps go unaddressed, and return on investment remains impossible to demonstrate.

Research shows that '*96% of learning happens in workflow*', yet most systems optimise for the remaining 4% that doesn't.

A Neural Network Architecture aligns with the 96%. Instead of a centralised hub pushing training, the neural core circulates insights, standards, and proven patterns that teams pull into their work as needed. Functional learning teams don't deliver courses but embed capability development into the tasks people already perform.

A central nervous system provides coherence through standards, governance, and shared resources, whilst distributed neurons (teams across functions) adapt knowledge to their specific challenges and feed lessons back to strengthen the entire system. Learning pathways ensure successful patterns spread, whilst failed experiments fade quickly.

Simon's agent marketplace operates this way in practice. When a finance team builds an AI solution that works, it isn't documented in a training module three months later; it's immediately migrated to the shared marketplace. The compliance team then adapts it to their context within days. The learning rate finally matches the change velocity because the model allows continuous insight transfer.

This is the structural transformation Systemic Learning facilitates, from centralised delivery to distributed intelligence, from scheduled programmes to continuous circulation, from functional silos to cross-boundary adaptation.

When learning sits inside work rather than around it, capability develops in line with business demands.

## The Leadership Evolution This Demands

*"Leadership has a critical role in evolving a firm's learning culture,"* Simon believes. *"That's why we're embedding AI expectations into our leadership expectations: creative problem-solving, psychological safety, continuous learning, curiosity."*

The shift from treating AI as a separate initiative to embedding it as a leadership expectation transforms the way capability is developed.

Individual capability matters only when leaders model and support it. Leadership modelling means little without embedding it into how work gets done, measured, and rewarded.

Leaders can no longer win by trying to be the smartest person in the room. They must become the orchestrator who makes the room smarter, who develops *Conductor Capabilities*, and Systemic Learning is to how you do it — whilst practicing transparent decision-making.

**Measuring Learning Rate:** The Antidote to Lehman's Mistake

Charles reframed learning measurements at Reuters. *"I implemented the 70:20:10 learning approach not to cut costs, but to accelerate and speed to productivity."*

By aligning L&D success with business performance metrics, he focused on changing outcomes, not chasing learning metrics. *"Our customer service team was struggling with retention and low customer satisfaction scores. I agreed with the Head of Customer Services that we would both tie our bonuses to an improvement in the satisfaction score. Few understood why we would take the risk, but simply pushing more learning was not the answer."*

They achieved their 3% improvement target within nine months through aligned collaboration between HR and the Customer

Services team. The impact on learning spend was equally revealing, *"Over five years, training spend dropped by 70%. That wasn't the goal, but by focusing on performance improvement, we were ruthless about only approving training that moved the business in the required direction."*

This is impactful because it highlights that learning budget decreased whilst business outcomes improved. Great evidence that learning effectiveness correlates with business relevance and application, not volume or investment.

Designing learning this way reframes it from a cost to a capability, and it demands entirely different metrics. Completion rates or satisfaction scores measure activity, not capability. The 'Learning Rate' formula measures whether the learning rate matches or exceeds change velocity, and that requires tracking how quickly people develop judgement that improves business outcomes.

## Learning Rate Scorecard

Measuring completion rates and satisfaction are the perfect ways to hide learning debt. To eliminate debt, you must measure its antidote, which is the rate of learning:

- **Learning Rate**: time from exposure to autonomous capability
- **Application Rate**: first-time-right percentage
- **Decision Rework Rate**: % of decisions needing reversal

Track three metrics revealing learning rate: time from exposure to autonomous capability (target: 50% reduction in 90 days), first-time-right percentage (target: >80% within two weeks), and decision rework rate (target: <20% requiring reversal).

When these improve, you're reducing learning debt and building judgement capital. This matters because when everyone accesses the same models, the organisation that develops human capability fastest will capture the advantage.

But Simon recognises the real race isn't against competitors; it's against AI's rate of advancement. *"We have a relatively narrow window to see what is true today and what can be predicted in the near term. AI capability is compounding exponentially, so our learning system needs to compound as fast, and traditional metrics won't tell me if we are winning that race,"* he explains.

## Your Next Move

Select one active AI initiative. Map backwards: Start with the desired results, identify the critical tasks that deliver them, then pinpoint the capability gaps preventing execution.

Design and test three integration points: one deliberate practice opportunity, one peer-learning mechanism that doesn't require meetings, and one reusable artefact that travels across teams.

Review learning-velocity indicators: time to clarity; first-time-right rates; rework frequency, alongside one business metric. Adjust based on what works for your business situation.

Repeat this cycle weekly because each iteration builds Systemic Learning that compounds rather than episodic training that fades.

## What Changes When Learning Rate Matches Rate of Change

Organisations that succeed with AI will rebuild learning, so capability develops where and when the work needs it. Neural Network Architecture solves what centralised programmes cannot by circulating working patterns immediately across teams.

Increasing the rate of learning is not about deploying better courses or more engaging content. It's about ensuring capability develops where and when work demands it. Central coordination no longer pushes programmes but circulates insights. Functional teams embed development into the workflow rather than deliver standalone training. Leaders evolve from experts to orchestrators who help others become smarter together.

When architecture, principles, leadership, and measurement align, the learning rate finally exceeds the rate of change. Capability debt is eliminated instead of accumulated. This is the fundamental shift from being comprehensively trained yet fundamentally unprepared to being systematically capable and continuously adapting.

The window for this transformation is narrowing as AI accelerates. The gap between your current learning architecture and the pace of change is widening.

The organisations that thrive by 2030 won't be those with better training, but those with a framework of Systemic Learning that compounds capability as fast as AI accelerates change.

*'Are your people solving problems faster than new problems appear?'*

If not, you need to apply the Systemic Learning principles to everything your team, function, or business does.

**Ritual:** Weekly Learning Extraction (30 minutes per team)

**Metric:** Learning Rate > Change Rate (Time to Clarity ↓ / First-Time-Right % ↑ / Decision Rework ↓)

**If You Remember One Thing:** Systemic Learning, the capability that develops through work, not around it, is the architecture that keeps learning rate ahead of change velocity in the AI era.

**Where This Takes You Next:** We will now explore leading transformation without losing trust and Adaptive Learning as a leadership capability, and together, how they help leaders build capability at scale.

CHAPTER 9

# LEADING TRANSFORMATION WITHOUT ERODING TRUST

## *You can't preserve trust if people don't see their future within the change*

### The Trust Dilemma

AI-related change has created unprecedented uncertainty. Many leaders still believe communication plans are the answer, but trust isn't built through words; it's built when people see evidence through principles and values lived under pressure.

A pattern that holds true is that trust is linked to how leaders choose to view their people. Consider your team and ask yourself if they are:

- Costs and resources used to achieve company targets?
- Or valuable capabilities to develop and elevate?

This is the choice every CEO and leader must face: optimise or develop. The choice will influence the outcome of your organisation's trust levels.

Major technology companies have all made a consistent pattern visible: large-scale workforce reductions alongside multi-billion-dollar AI investments. From back-office automation to AI-led product platforms, organisations are framing these moves as 'efficiency' to fund expansion into AI.

The message this clearly sends: AI-related cost savings matter more than people, and trust then erodes as AI is seen as a replacement rather than something that elevates their potential.

## The Speed Paradox Becomes Real

Every technology wave that has arrived to date has, with it, disrupted work. But AI intensifies disruption to a level that challenges the very foundations of leadership. Earlier, automation largely displaced manual roles, but at the same time brought new opportunities that people could anticipate and adapt to. AI accelerates this change and uniquely displaces cognitive work more than manual roles.

This fuels fear for those whose expertise is now being automated. Will knowledge, identity, and value become irrelevant or obsolete at exponential speed?

The speed paradox discussed in Chapter 8 is now becoming more vivid. But learning rate depends on something deeper: trust. When people don't trust that their expertise will remain valued, they resist learning. When they don't trust leaders' decisions, they won't execute them. Speed without trust creates motion, not transformation. Leaders must balance these dynamics, actively manage change, quickly articulate strategy, and build human capability to match the pace of change. If the gap widens too far, trust collapses into that space.

Caroline Barth, Syngenta Group's CHRO, chose the development path in an industry where technology is already transforming agriculture as fundamentally as mechanisation once did. Syngenta's CEO captured this vision, "*Data is the new tractor*." Just as tractors revolutionised agricultural productivity, AI now promises an equally disruptive transformation.

Caroline understands that connecting a fast-moving digital strategy to a slower-moving human foundation depends on trust. Trust that expertise will still be valued, developed, and supported through change. *"For every $1 invested in technology, invest at least $1, if not more, in capability development, cultural adaptation, change management, and trust preservation."*

This 1:1 ratio matters because an AI tool can be installed in months, yet building people's skills, confidence, and trust in those systems takes years. When companies spend exponentially on technology and reduce spend on people, the effects will be felt in the long term.

People notice everything. When million-dollar AI platforms are approved instantly, whilst training programmes stall, it's clear that technology matters more than people. Employees already perceive AI might replace them, so watching this display only further collapses trust.

## Trust: Your Greatest Transformation Asset

In the race for speed, most leaders underestimate trust's power to determine whether transformation succeeds or stalls. This chapter establishes trust as the foundation, not one of many building blocks, but the load-bearing structure on which everything else depends.

Research combining relational psychology and organisational data shows that trust is not an emotional state but an operational stance, a '*willingness to act under uncertainty when outcomes cannot be fully verified.*' Without this foundation, moving to readiness (Chapter 10) and then results (Chapter 11) is premature. Systematic coordination requires trust — trust between peers, within teams, and in the values and integrity of senior leadership.

I believe trust is the greatest transformation asset because the most significant barrier to AI implementation isn't technology, but people's trust in leadership judgement and intent, in the process, in the technology, and in each other to create orchestrated change.

Trust incentivises skills development, collaboration between functions, acceptance of technology, and each other's part in shared ownership of a vision. Far from being aspirational, it has to become your reality. When trust erodes, capability development stalls, collaboration fragments, and transformation becomes a failure statistic.

Build trust systematically, and systematic coordination becomes probable, not just a hope.

## Competing Leadership Pressures

To set the context for leadership success, let's first consider the current reality and the challenges it presents to leaders. AI transformation sits at the intersection of competing pressures that consistently test a leader's ability to create trust:

**External pressures:** market disruption, competitive threats, geopolitical uncertainty, customer expectations, and relentless technological change demanding response.

**Internal pressures:** people's uncertainty about their career futures colliding with organisational forces, business functions optimising in isolation, demands for efficiency overriding relationship preservation, and speed requirements contradicting collaborative culture.

Leaders, unfortunately, get caught in the middle. They feel pressure to deliver speed whilst preserving trust, drive efficiency whilst inspiring confidence, and to accelerate change whilst building capability. This is a significant challenge and is the reason why I'm consistently asked:

*'How can leaders navigate these competing pressures whilst keeping people engaged and confident in their futures?'*

To answer that, I turn to the Trust Equation, developed by Maister, Green, and Galford, a simple but powerful lens for understanding what's at stake:

$$\overset{\text{Trust}}{T} = \frac{\overset{\text{Credibility}}{C} + \overset{\text{Reliability}}{R} + \overset{\text{Intimacy}}{I}}{\underset{\text{Self-Orientation}}{S}}$$

Use the Trust Equation as a diagnostic lens for AI-driven change. Each component becomes a stress point under competing pressures. When speed and efficiency dominate decisions, self-orientation rises and trust weakens. The perception that people's futures matter less than organisational efficiency destroys trust faster than technical excellence can rebuild it.

Trust determines whether employees interpret disruption as an investment or a threat, whether they choose to engage or withdraw. Without it, even technically flawless AI implementations fail because people resist, skills don't develop, and coordination fractures. This makes trust non-negotiable.

## Trust Is Non-Negotiable

When AI transformations fall short of expectations, I see the same pattern: Self-orientation triggers a confidence collapse. The narrative emphasises restructuring and efficiency gains, and employees conclude that decisions serve cost-cutting rather than their future. Self-orientation spikes in the Trust Equation. Trust falls faster than technical excellence can rebuild it.

This harsh reality must guide every leader managing AI-driven change. Recognising and addressing this dynamic becomes essential to preserving talent and achieving sustainable transformation.

Rebecca Snow, Global People & Organisation VP at Mars Incorporated, addresses this urgency. "*Trust isn't aspirational, but a necessity. By measuring trust directly, we hold leaders accountable for fostering genuine care and well-being. Aligned to our values, transparent communication and humility build the trust that makes transformation possible.*"

She warns that without visible leadership engagement and ongoing dialogue about "*what's in it for me*" and "*why should we evolve*", organisations risk eroding trust and therefore losing their talent. Rebecca explains, "*Large established firms are rarely ready for scaling AI in the same way as frontier firms or start-ups are. Structures, data, processes, and legacy systems must adapt, which takes time. We must use this time to tell the story honestly, to place humans at the centre, and map our journey to sustained success.*"

As Chapter 8 established, realising AI-powered growth ambitions requires capability development embedded in the flow of work, woven into daily operations. When AI deployment outpaces learning and trust-building, engagement, culture, and performance inevitably erode.

Caroline captures the dimension precisely: "*You cannot digitally transform an organisation faster than you can build the trust required to sustain it.*"

When change accelerates beyond people's capacity to adapt, AI-driven efficiency might generate short-term gains, but long-term damage becomes inevitable. Once this happens, trust cannot be rebuilt through reassurance alone. It must be earned through upskilling, internal mobility, visible career pathways, and growth opportunities that turn uncertainty into engagement. When employees see how their skills align with the future organisation, they view disruption as an investment rather than a threat.

This explains why organisations that succeed invest between one and three times more in people than in technology. It isn't just trust-preservation mathematics; behaviour change and capability development take time, repetition, and sustained investment. Organisations that underinvest signal that cost matters more than capability. Self-orientation then dominates the Trust Equation, trust erodes, and technology remains under-realised.

The difference between success and failure hinges on whether leaders build visible futures for people inside the change. Mars demonstrates this through values lived under pressure. Syngenta Group demonstrates it through systematic investment in capability. Both recognise that AI transformation without trust preservation joins the statistical majority of AI failures.

Where does trust break first? Rarely all at once, but not in isolation either.

During AI transformations, trust usually erodes through distinct pressure points. What makes this moment dangerous is that several of them tend to activate at the same time, amplifying their impact.

## Three Tensions That Test Trust

Trust is frequently tested through three recurring tensions that can surface simultaneously.

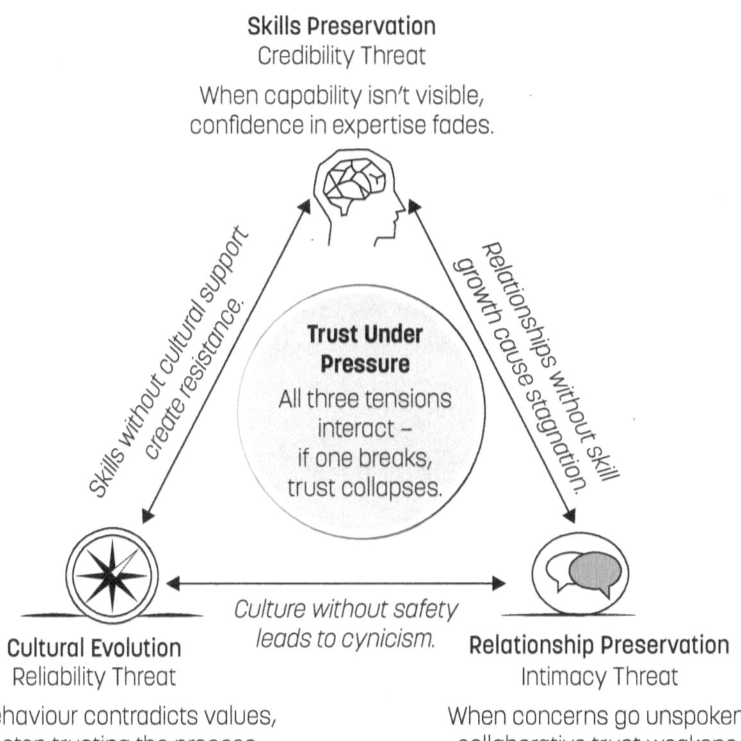


### 1. Skills Preservation (Credibility Threat)

**Signal:** Leaders stuck in task execution. Root cause analysis absent. People unsure how their expertise translates to AI-enabled work.

**Impact:** AI handles execution. People need diagnostic capability before automation eliminates the practice that builds it. Without visible career pathways showing how skills evolve, credibility collapses, and people lose confidence in their ability to contribute.

**Caroline's approach:** *"Root cause analysis is going to be critical because when we rely more on AI and experience problems, I'm going to look to our leaders to solve the core problems."* She's building diagnostic capability through structured problem analysis, not by hoping people figure it out on their own.

**Rebecca's approach:** "*We have focused our efforts on areas that provide growth and increased effectiveness for Associates (employees). This shifts the focus from any concern about replacement to the tangible benefit of growth, preserving invaluable experience whilst building new, critical capacities. A clear roadmap is designed to guide the transition, ensuring team members have the required path and support to advance impact.*"

**Your move:** Add a 30-minute 'root cause round' to weekly operations. One problem, one diagnosis, one reusable fix documented. Show people they're moving up the value chain.

### 2. Cultural Evolution (Reliability Threat)

**Signal:** Consensus culture slows decisions. Values are invisible under pressure. Performance urgency feels like abandoning collaboration.

**Impact:** Collaborative cultures value consensus. AI transformation demands speed. This creates whiplash: maintain relationships whilst accelerating decisions. Without principle-guided acceleration, reliability collapses, and people perceive values as negotiable under pressure.

**Caroline's tension:** *"In a compassionate company, it feels countercultural to assess the top thirty positions creating the most value and challenge whether these people are evolving at the pace needed. But we have an obligation to act, sensitively and with resolve."* High expectations inevitably create tension, but when combined with total accountability and psychological safety, they produce a responsible workforce. Caroline's approach is to form small cross-functional teams with end-to-end accountability and a high degree of collaboration, structures that preserve compassion whilst enabling speed.

**Rebecca's approach:** *"Our Five Principles speak as much to how we do business as to what we deliver. There isn't a trade-off between performance and culture; profit sustains Freedom, but we pursue it with Responsibility and Mutuality. Those principles are timeless. When we explain tough changes through them, people don't feel at the whim of a passing leader; they feel part of a hundred-year arc."*

**Your move:** Document three decisions where speed matters and explain how you'll protect people through them. Make principles visible and act on them. Publish 'principled accelerators' that, despite speed, still preserve values.

### 3. Relationship Preservation (Intimacy Threat)

**Signal:** Silence or blame around imperfect tools. People are hiding their frustrations. Feedback doesn't flow.

**Impact:** Technology deployed without psychological safety destroys intimacy. When people can't speak honestly about what's not working, frustration stays hidden until it erupts as resistance or resignation. The relationship between leaders and teams erodes in silence.

**Caroline's approach:** She understood that imperfect AI tools could destroy relationships if frustrations remain hidden. She therefore created explicit feedback channels with a clear commitment. *"When we roll out an agent, we know it will be imperfect. If you use it and hate it, tell us what didn't work and let's co-create solutions together."* This is about transparent expectation setting. Caroline also recognised that AI should not be layered onto existing processes. When something doesn't work, the critical question becomes which part of the process needs redesigning.

What preserves trust here is not perfection, but visible response; when feedback leads to action, frustration becomes information rather than disengagement.

**Rebecca's approach:** With any transformation effort, Mars increases senior leader presence and communication not only through town halls and pulse checks, but through working sessions, 'surgeries', or communities of practice where people could ask hard questions or learn in a safe environment. *"We commit to being in the room where anxiety is highest. Not to have all the answers, but to be present whilst we figure it out together. That presence matters more than perfect messaging."* When leaders show up in uncomfortable spaces, relationships deepen rather than fray.

**Your move:** Create a feedback channel for one AI tool with a commitment to respond. Make three visible fixes based on input this month. Show feedback matters through action, not just collection.

## Why These Tensions Interact

Skills preservation without cultural support creates resistance. People develop new capabilities, but culture punishes their use, creating inconsistency that undermines reliability. Cultural evolution without relationship safety creates cynicism. Performance urgency without intimacy feels like internal optimisation, spiking self-orientation. Preserving relationships without skills development leads to stagnation. Intimacy without credibility becomes empty reassurance that transformation will somehow succeed despite capability gaps.

The breakthrough is recognising these aren't sequential challenges but one integrated system requiring simultaneous resolution through systematic trust verification.

## Trust Checkpoints

Whilst researching AI transformation failures, one discipline was consistently missing: systematic verification that trust keeps pace with technological progress. Traditional methods track technical delivery, yet sustainable transformation tracks trust preservation and also capability building.

Caroline shared a memorable analogy: *"Nobody calls a piece of music a failure because of a few off notes. You hear it, adjust, and play better next time. Off notes are just information, nothing more."*

That idea can reshape how you think about mistakes within a transformation. Instead of relying solely on technical milestones, leaders can use Trust Checkpoints or short pauses to verify whether implementation is strengthening or eroding human potential, relationships, and organisational confidence.

Here is my simple 45-minute review to make trust measurable every month:

1. **Choose one live initiative** (5 minutes)
   Pick an active AI project, which could be a new agent, workflow, or decision tool.

2. **Score the four trust factors** (15 minutes)
   Rate each: 0 = eroding, 1 = neutral, 2 = building.

- **Credibility:** Do people feel more capable or more confused?
- **Reliability:** Under pressure, did we uphold values or default to efficiency?
- **Intimacy:** Can people speak honestly about what isn't working?
- **Self-Orientation:** Are we investing in people's futures or only in the system?

3. **Define one fix per low score** (15 minutes)

- Low credibility → run a short skill-building session.
- Low reliability → publish how principles guided a tough call.
- Low intimacy → open a feedback loop with visible fixes.
- High self-orientation → show tangible reinvestment in people, not tools.

4. **Assign ownership and document** (10 minutes)
   Name who acts and by when, and create the one-pager showing initiative name, scores, fixes, owners, and subsequent review date.

**5. Publish**

Make trust verification visible, not buried in leadership decks.

When teams see that trust is measured as deliberately as performance, transformation feels safe rather than threatening. These deliberate pauses prevent the speed trap of rushing ahead whilst trust quietly decays.

Trust checkpoints help shift trust from just a value, into a system that safeguards sustainable transformation.

## Building on Strategic Foundations: *Conductor Capabilities*

In Chapter 6, you developed the foundations for two of the four *Conductor Capabilities* that support strategic execution at AI speed:

**Judgement Under Ambiguity** introduced how to set strategic rhythm, remembering when to pause for reflection and when to accelerate for learning. Building the personal skills that come with your *Action Centres* and *Gut*, these then became helpful at the organisational level, using the AI Board Consult's four voices and broadening considerations required for robust judgement.

**Enterprise Orchestration** was introduced as a guiding principle: the need to design for decisions to travel cleanly across functions. You explored elements such as decision rights, flexible integration points, and the shift from silo metrics to Adjusted Value. The deeper leadership skills required to sustain orchestration at scale will be developed in the next chapter. Together these chapters trace how principles first surface, then mature into leadership capabilities.

These capabilities form the strategic core of *Conductor leadership*, but they're not sufficient for leaders managing scaled transformations. Orchestrating strategic decisions is, of course, critical, but sustaining that orchestration during months of transformation work (whilst preserving trust and building capability) requires an additional two capabilities:

**The Two Sustaining Capabilities**
Helping set direction and enable coherent action

**Trust Stewardship**

**Making trust operational and visible.**
Ensures people feel their future is protected as the organisation accelerates through AI-driven change.

WHY IT MATTERS

Trust is the foundation for coordinated transformation.
Without it, speed creates fear, learning stalls, and decisions lose followability.

*Confidence in leadership intent. Safety to adapt. Commitment under uncertainty.*

**Adaptive Learning**

**Building capability faster than complexity grows.**
Creates continuous improvement through feedback, experimentation, and shared learning.

WHY IT MATTERS

Learning tightens feedback loops, amplifies capability and keeps teams ahead of accelerating change.

*Capability grows. Confidence compounds. Progress becomes sustainable.*

TRUST STEADIES THE SYSTEM. LEARNING KEEPS IT MOVING.

We now focus on these additional two enablers to help you scale and sustain your impact whilst working under enterprise-wide AI transformation pressures.

## Trust Stewardship

Conductors operationalise trust by managing all elements in the Trust Equation.

They build Credibility through sustained skill development, Reliability through consistent behaviour, and Intimacy through psychological safety that enables challenge without fear. At the same time, they keep Self-Interest low by demonstrating that people's futures matter as much as short-term performance.

Trust stewardship also means embedding responsible AI governance: bias checks, model-risk controls, transparency standards, and kill-switch protocols. Leaders use trust checkpoints to test whether progress is strengthening or eroding human potential rather than assuming impact after the fact.

### Observable Behaviours Include:

- Can leaders point to decisions where both data and values guided the choice?
- Are trust thresholds tracked and acted on monthly rather than deferred to annual reviews?
- Does every AI initiative have a named owner for transparency, bias control, and rollback?

Trust Stewardship is not about making people feel safe. It is about designing systems where acting under uncertainty is rational, mutual, and recognised, and where resilience emerges collectively rather than being demanded individually.

### Adaptive Learning

Conductors build learning into the flow of work through short feedback loops and structured experimentation.

They model humble learning through reverse mentoring and measure deep adoption, confident use, and better judgement rather than surface activity or login metrics.

They make capability development every leader's responsibility, not just HR's. They establish weekly root-cause rounds to explore one issue, one diagnosis, and one reusable fix. They apply the People Proxy voice to ensure learning feels like an investment, not a burden.

When people feel safe to experiment, feedback loops tighten. When loops tighten, capability grows. And when capability grows, confidence compounds — accelerating both learning and trust.

**Observable Behaviours:**

- Do they embed learning into daily operations rather than treating it as a side project?

- Do people feel safe surfacing what isn't working early and openly?
- Can they point to lessons reused across functions, not just within one team?

Taken together, these behaviours only deliver their full impact when Adaptive Learning is combined to create an integrated system.

## The Four Capabilities as an Integrated System

AI-era leadership demands that all four *Conductor Capabilities must* operate as a single system:

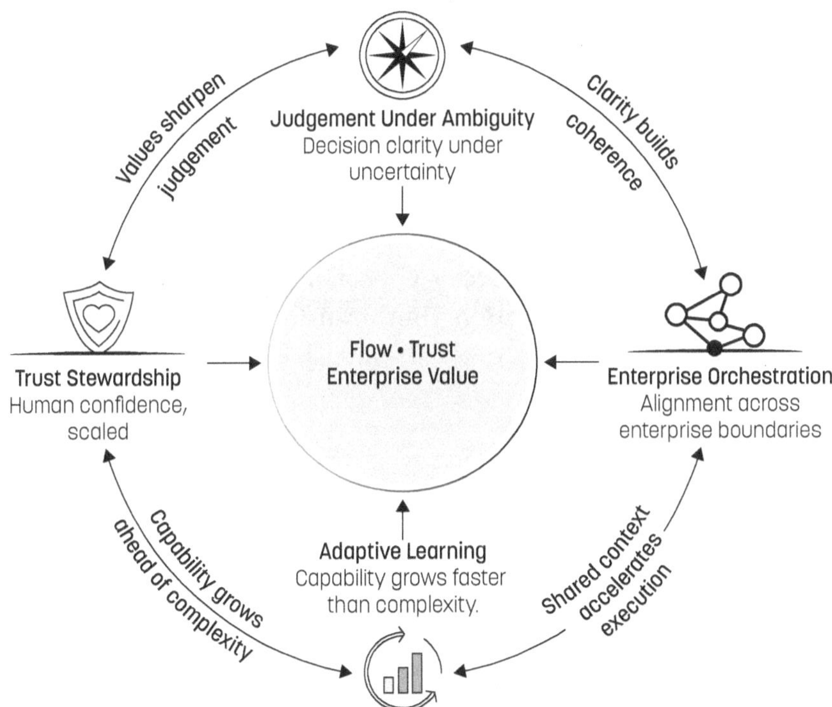


When Conductor Capabilities work in sync, leaders create flow, build trust, and accelerate enterprise value.

When integrated and applied consistently, these capabilities form the leadership circuitry of a networked organisation, one that senses, decides, and adapts through trust, rather than hierarchical control.

'Leadership' finally shifts from an individual performance focus to a focus on being a conductor of a system that learns as it leads. The shift is from authority to orchestration, from certainty to sensing, from performance to flow.

Those who master this transition transform AI from a technical upgrade into a cultural evolution, one where speed, trust, and humanity coexist in a single rhythm.

## From Individual Mastery to Conductor Capability

The four *Conductor Capabilities* define what effective AI-era leadership looks like at the system level — how you set rhythm, align boundaries, preserve trust, and accelerate learning. They become impactful when leaders and their teams develop the underlying skills that enable orchestration.

This requires a fundamental shift in how individuals work, not just how leaders lead. The *Conductor Capabilities* you've built create the conditions for transformation. But transformation only happens when people at every level evolve from task execution to judgement partnership with AI.

The skills evolution below shows what this means in practice — the shift from task era work to AI era capability that *Conductor leadership* enables and requires.

## Skills Evolution: From Tasks to Judgement

The capabilities we have been building facilitate a fundamental skill shift that represents career advancement rather than fear of replacement. This shift is empowering, but for the full benefit to be experienced, reflect during each moment or decision to assess whether you are working under the old leadership task era approach or shifting to the new:

| From (Task Era) | To (AI era) | What This Requires |
|---|---|---|
| Responding to symptoms | Root cause diagnosis | Analytical capability understanding underlying issues and designing sustainable solutions |
| Following procedures | Choosing which problems deserve solving | Strategic thinking about impact over activity |
| Tool operation | Partnership intelligence | Knowing when to trust or override AI recommendations and explain why |
| Applying AI to existing work | Reshaping work for partnership | Willingness to change processes, not just add tools |

Reshaping work to enable human-AI partnership, rather than just applying AI to existing processes, proves most difficult because it challenges organisational identity. The willingness to change separates organisations that augment human capability from those that automate towards mediocrity.

## Making the Shift Systematic

Individual skills evolution doesn't happen through osmosis. It requires systematic investment in capability development that makes the four *Conductor Capabilities* operational across the entire leadership population, not just for a few exceptional individuals.

Caroline's approach demonstrates how to build transformation readiness deliberately, creating the conditions where skills evolution can scale beyond individual heroics.

## Building Transformation Readiness Systematically

Before implementing rapid change, systematic foundation-building proves essential. Caroline's experience demonstrates this: *"We are offering a six-month AI executive education experience, similar to a mini-MBA on AI, for our most senior leaders. Whilst not mandatory, it will be clear that we expect all our leadership to become not only AI literate, but also to nurture the next generation of AI leaders. We need the top 1% of the organisation to have a shared language, goals, talent expectations, and speed of understanding."*

This investment serves multiple purposes beyond knowledge transfer. Shared language enables coordination. As Chapter 8 established, development must sit in the flow of work, not solely as HR's job. All leaders must treat talent development as a performance metric. This creates aligned expectations about talent performance and builds a foundation for cultural evolution.

Top-down mandates spike self-orientation in the Trust Equation, destroying the intimacy that collaborative culture creates. Instead, we must position capability-building as enabling what leaders already want: the ability to navigate transformation effectively whilst preserving what makes the organisation successful.

## The Leadership Evolution This Demands

Leadership in the AI era isn't about achieving perfect alignment, but about creating it dynamically. The strongest leaders don't wait for clarity; they create it through systematic investment in learning, trust, and cross-boundary collaboration.

As Caroline articulates, every function must "*step up so the whole can be jointly elevated.*" Leadership is no longer about controlling expertise within silos but enabling expertise to flow across them. The conductor mindset becomes the operating norm by coordinating through trust rather than authority and proving value through the outcomes others achieve.

Leaders who master this balance don't lose trust; they multiply it. Despite uncertainty and change, they turn anxiety into engagement, capability grows, and AI becomes an amplifier of human potential.

They make trust measurable, ensure values are visible even under pressure, and invest in personal growth so that **those they lead see themselves in the future they are building**.

Speed without trust limits success. Trust built systematically multiplies it.

This is the leadership evolution required to excel in an AI-driven environment:

- **credibility** through continuous learning and visible expertise
- **reliability** through consistent, values-based action under pressure
- **intimacy** through empathy and psychological safety at scale
- **low self-orientation** through investment in collective capability, not personal preservation

AI redefines leadership as the stewardship of trust at scale.

Leaders who design organisations where trust is verified, not assumed, will not only keep their best people, but also unlock their greatest potential.

You began building *Conductor Capabilities* in Chapter 6 with Judgement and Orchestration. This chapter completed the system with Trust and Learning.

Trust makes transformation possible, and readiness determines whether it lasts.

**Ritual:** Monthly Trust Threshold Review (45-minute checkpoint process)

**Metric:** Trust Pulse = (Credibility + Reliability + Intimacy) ÷ Self-Orientation. Score each component 0-2. Higher numerator = better. Lower denominator = better. Aim for a combined score above 4.0. Also track: Time to Capability on New Tasks + Adjusted Value (converged outcomes).

**If You Remember One Thing:** You cannot preserve trust if people don't see a future for themselves inside the change. AI transformation succeeds when investment in capability is visible, and values are lived under pressure. People must see evidence that they will thrive, not just survive.

**Where This Takes You Next:** Trust alone is not enough. Even when people believe in the intent of change, execution fails if the organisation cannot coordinate strategy, operations, and people under pressure. Next, we examine whether your organisation has built the integrated capabilities required for convergence — the readiness foundations that determine whether trust translates into results.

# PART IV

# Reshape for Flow

## (Leading the Organisation)

*Reshape work around flows (outcomes), not functions. Create structures where technology, trust, and talent move together. Replace sequential hand-offs with simultaneous collaboration so human and AI intelligence travels freely through the organisation.*

CHAPTER 10

# READINESS TO RUN CONVERGED FLOWS

# *Coordinate timing despite AI speed*

Readiness assessments often lie.

The most expensive example I have witnessed cost a firm significantly more than CHF 600m. I was leading a workstream within this organisation's third attempt at an enterprise-wide ERP implementation. They had all the required capabilities, adequate budget, and leadership aligned with the vision. My team was commissioned after they recognised 'change management' had been underinvested, and the fundamental coordination gaps were immediately clear.

Yet my workstream was out of sync with the other business areas, a microcosm of the dysfunction that would later see the programme's budget explode from CHF 800 million to over CHF 1.8 billion. Preparing people for end-to-end processes that hadn't been built, or building training for non-existent workflows, was a symptom of the infamous 'big bang' approach that forced customisation over alignment.

Leadership meetings (with exco members) consumed hours examining technical minutiae, yet missed critical big picture misalignments and challenges that were actually the root cause of the programme crisis. We were building our own Airbus A380, part by part, without ensuring compatibility.

The lack of integrated coordination had direct and costly consequences. The ultimate proof came in the form of multi-year delays and a line in the company's annual report of a CHF 600 million impairment charge.

The failure wasn't technical capability, but coordination. There was no system in place to keep strategy, operations, and people moving together in sync under pressure.

Traditional readiness assessments will never catch this. Individual components might have green ticks, but they miss the fact that coordination capability is red.

In an AI-driven enterprise, misalignment is even more damaging. As systems accelerate decisions and increase interdependence, gaps between authority, accountability, and judgement propagate faster and become harder to correct.

This is not a systems problem alone. It exposes a leadership gap. The instincts that once helped leaders succeed no longer create coherence when work becomes continuous and AI-driven. Incremental shifts no longer surface. Orchestration now demands that leaders relinquish control while taking greater ownership of judgement, coherence, and outcome. Becoming an orchestrator is not a skill upgrade. It is the continuation of the identity shift we started in Chapter 1.

## The Readiness Illusion

This is the readiness illusion most leaders face. There is an appearance of readiness, but when coordination pressure hits, everything stalls.

Research into AI transformation failures is nuanced, but we know failure rates may be as high as 95% and that technology and AI sophistication are not the main reasons for this alarmingly high statistic. The gap between component readiness and coordination capability explains this pattern.

As Howard Yu, the LEGO® Professor of Management and Innovation at IMD Business School, observes, *"We repeatedly see a pattern I call 'efficient mediocrity' where organisations optimise every component beautifully, but cannot coordinate across boundaries. They achieve local excellence whilst enterprise value fragments. Component metrics look green whilst coordination capability remains absent."*

Component-focused approaches dominate enterprise transformations yet consistently fail to deliver successful implementation. Genuine readiness requires systematic capability building that asks fundamentally different questions such as: '*Are we ready to coordinate the people and technology-related variables at the required speed when AI accelerates all three simultaneously?*'

The systematic capability-building principles we saw demonstrated in Chapter 9 create robust resilience. Systemic learning, strategic talent development, and cultural evolution produce actual readiness instead of superficial preparation. Organisations with systematic capabilities through approaches like SPAR navigate complexities that others find impossible.

The distinction between component completion and coordination capability led me to research the requirements for integrated capabilities and how to assess them before deployment pressure exposes gaps. This insight became the foundation for the *Readiness Trinity*, a measure of an organisation's ability to keep three rhythms aligned: strategy, operations, and people.

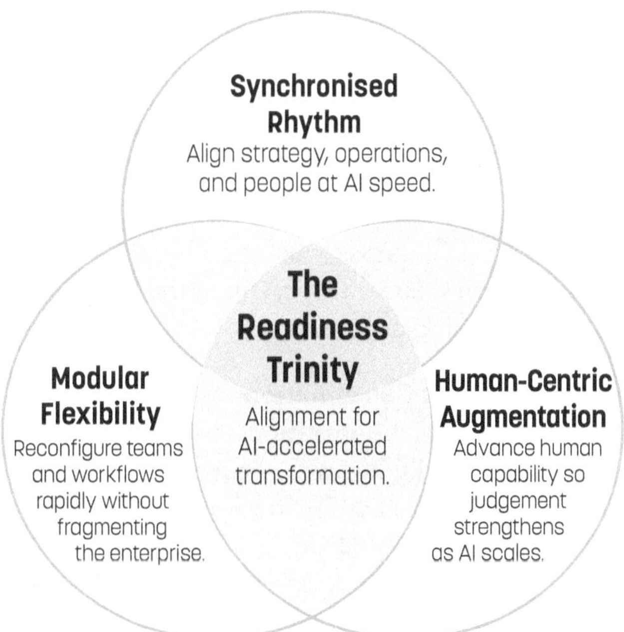


AI accelerates organisational rhythms.
*The Readiness Trinity* keeps them coherent under pressure.

Before explaining what the Trinity measures, diagnose where your organisation stands right now. This takes 10 minutes. Answer based on evidence from the last quarter, not aspirations.

## The Trinity Readiness Scan: A Quick Diagnostic

This scan provides a quick diagnostic of your Trinity integration: not a validated research instrument, but a practical tool for identifying where coordination gaps likely exist before deployment pressure exposes them catastrophically.

### Scoring Instructions:

For each question, score based on current reality evidenced in recent decisions:

- **Yes** (2 points): strong evidence from past quarter, multiple examples
- **Partially** (1 point): some evidence, inconsistent across organisation
- **No** (0 points): little to no evidence, capability absent

**Maximum Score:** 30 points

Answer honestly. 'Partially' indicates gaps requiring attention before scaling deployment.

## Synchronised Rhythm

Can your organisation keep Strategic, Operational, and Human Clocks moving together under AI acceleration?

1. **Strategic-Operational Coordination**
   When strategy pivots, do operations articulate specifically which changes to their workflows will occur within two weeks, whilst executing those changes within 30 days?
   □ Yes (2) | □ Partially (1) | □ No (0)

**2. Strategic-Human Coordination**
Can you trace each strategic priority to both the operational metrics that teams use daily AND to specific capability development initiatives supporting those teams?
□ Yes (2) | □ Partially (1) | □ No (0)

**3. Operational-Human Coordination**
When operational processes change, do affected teams receive capability development within the same month (not months later)?
□ Yes (2) | □ Partially (1) | □ No (0)

**4. Clock Advancement Review**
Do your quarterly reviews show all three clocks advancing (strategy evolving, operations improving, people developing) rather than progress concentrated in one or two whilst another lags?
□ Yes (2) | □ Partially (1) | □ No (0)

**5. Cross-Functional Coordination Speed**
When competing demands create time pressure, do teams coordinate priorities across functions quickly (within 48 hours) without requiring escalation?
□ Yes (2) | □ Partially (1) | □ No (0)

**Synchronised Rhythm Subtotal: _____ / 10**

## Human-Centric Augmentation

Is the Human Clock keeping pace with Strategic and Operational acceleration through AI partnership?

**6. AI Partnership Quality**
Can employees explain specifically how AI changed their decision quality, with examples of when they override AI recommendations and why, based on judgement?
□ Yes (2) | □ Partially (1) | □ No (0)

**7. Investment Ratio Evidence**
For every dollar spent on AI technology, can you demonstrate spending between one and three dollars on people development,

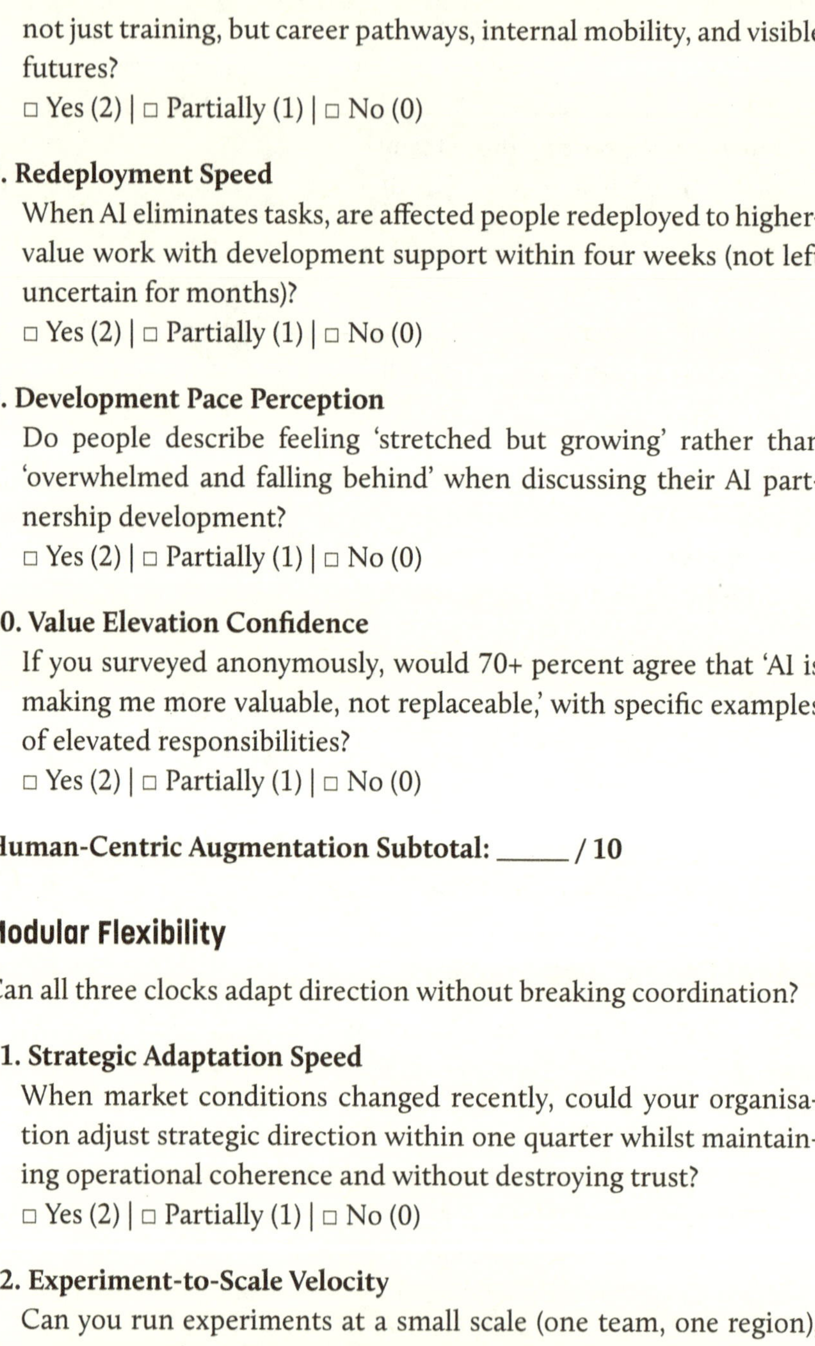

not just training, but career pathways, internal mobility, and visible futures?

□ Yes (2) | □ Partially (1) | □ No (0)

**8. Redeployment Speed**

When AI eliminates tasks, are affected people redeployed to higher-value work with development support within four weeks (not left uncertain for months)?

□ Yes (2) | □ Partially (1) | □ No (0)

**9. Development Pace Perception**

Do people describe feeling 'stretched but growing' rather than 'overwhelmed and falling behind' when discussing their AI partnership development?

□ Yes (2) | □ Partially (1) | □ No (0)

**10. Value Elevation Confidence**

If you surveyed anonymously, would 70+ percent agree that 'AI is making me more valuable, not replaceable,' with specific examples of elevated responsibilities?

□ Yes (2) | □ Partially (1) | □ No (0)

**Human-Centric Augmentation Subtotal: _____ / 10**

## Modular Flexibility

Can all three clocks adapt direction without breaking coordination?

**11. Strategic Adaptation Speed**

When market conditions changed recently, could your organisation adjust strategic direction within one quarter whilst maintaining operational coherence and without destroying trust?

□ Yes (2) | □ Partially (1) | □ No (0)

**12. Experiment-to-Scale Velocity**

Can you run experiments at a small scale (one team, one region), measure results, then scale successful approaches or kill unsuccessful ones within six months?

□ Yes (2) | □ Partially (1) | □ No (0)

**13. Bottom-Up Innovation**

Do teams propose new ways of working based on AI capabilities they discover, or do they wait for central direction before adapting practices?

□ Yes (2) | □ Partially (1) | □ No (0)

**14. Role Adaptation Capability**

When roles change due to AI capabilities, do people adapt within three months whilst maintaining performance (not requiring 6-to-12 months of transition)?

□ Yes (2) | □ Partially (1) | □ No (0)

**15. Resource Reallocation Agility**

Can you redirect resources from declining to growing priorities within one quarter without requiring complete restructuring or 18-month transformation programmes?

□ Yes (2) | □ Partially (1) | □ No (0)

**Modular Flexibility Subtotal: _____ / 10**

**TOTAL TRINITY INTEGRATION SCORE: _____ / 30**

Write down your scores. We will come back to these later. You can also refer to Appendix F when ready to consider potential actions for improvement.

## The Readiness Trinity: What your scores reveal

Howard Yu's research through IMD's Future Readiness Indicator has tracked companies across financial fundamentals, innovation investment, and organisational agility over more than a decade. His research reveals a persistent pattern: "*High performers demonstrate integrated capabilities rather than component excellence. Organisations excelling on individual metrics such as strong technology or high training completion, frequently fail when convergence demands coordination. The companies that succeeded had something different; they kept multiple organisational rhythms synchronised even as AI accelerated all of them simultaneously.*"

The Trinity Readiness framework emerged from understanding what enables this synchronisation. The fifteen questions you just answered measure the foundations that determine whether coordination holds under AI acceleration.

## The Three Clocks: Understanding the Rhythms of Convergence

The Three Clocks you assessed measure how strategy, operations, and people move together under AI acceleration. Every organisation runs these three clocks, each ticking at its own pace, each essential for survival. Let's examine each of the clocks and their rhythms:

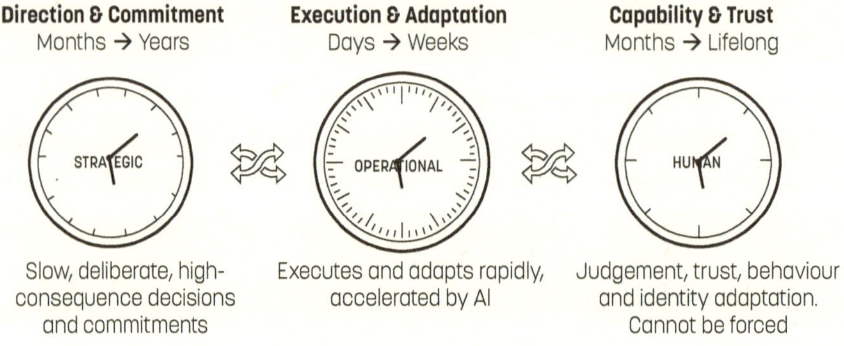


These three rhythms underpin the Readiness Trinity.

**The Strategic Clock** measures how quickly your organisation can sense shifts, reframe opportunity, and commit to direction. It sets the rhythm of choice. In the past, this clock could tick slowly through annual plans and quarterly reviews. Today, AI compresses strategic windows from years to months. Push it too fast, however, and strategy becomes whiplash: constant pivots without follow-through that disorient the organisation.

**The Operational Clock** tracks execution speed, i.e. how quickly work moves, products ship, and value reaches customers. AI can accelerate this dramatically through automation and prediction. But operational speed without strategic clarity produces efficient chaos: doing the wrong things faster.

**The Human Clock** reflects how quickly people adapt, learn, and emotionally process change. It is the slowest, most fragile, and most ignored rhythm. AI has not accelerated trust, learning, or cultural change. These still require time, repetition, and psychological safety.

In my ERP failure example, the Strategic Clock raced ahead with executive commitment to transformation. The Operational Clock tried to match it with aggressive deployment timelines. But the Human Clock couldn't keep pace, and people were preparing for workflows that didn't exist, learning systems that kept changing, adapting faster than trust or capability could develop. The clocks desynchronised and the programme felt the strain.

AI removes the margin for drift. When strategic cycles change, misaligned rhythms no longer slow progress but fracture it. The answer isn't forcing the same speed, it's designed convergence:

- Strategy sets clear guardrails for faster execution.
- Operations embeds learning loops that develop capability.
- Human insight informs strategic choice before momentum locks.

This is *readiness to run converged flows*: not everything moving at the same speed, but everything moving in the same direction with timing that respects both AI acceleration and human reality.

## The Readiness Trinity: Three Foundations Enabling Coherence

### 1. Synchronised Rhythm

The ability to keep all three clocks moving together, fast enough to capture opportunity, deliberate enough to preserve judgement, coordinated enough to prevent fragmentation. Synchronised Rhythm coordinates across different tempos (The Strategic Clock moves slower than the Operational, and the Human Clock slower still), so no clock becomes a bottleneck or races ahead unsustainably.

**Connection to SPAR:** Your personal rhythm and team coordination capabilities built in Chapters 1-4 allow you to decide when to pause for reflection and when to accelerate, setting the appropriate pace for all three clocks.

**Without it:** Desynchronisation compounds until transformation stalls. Strategy accelerates whilst operations lag (destroying credibility); or operations deploy whilst people resist (wasting investment); or people demand certainty whilst strategy must remain fluid (missing market windows).

### 2. Human-Centric Augmentation

The capability to keep the Human Clock advancing through AI deployment, preserving expertise whilst enabling partnership, maintaining judgement whilst accelerating analysis. As Howard observes, *"The organisations that succeed systematically invest in elevating human capability alongside technology. The ratio matters, and we consistently see 1:1 or 1:3 spending on people development relative to technology investment. This isn't altruism; it's the mathematics of coordination under acceleration."*

**Connection to SPAR**: This emerged from Chapter 9's trust preservation, maintaining psychological safety, Adaptive Learning embedding development in daily operations, and investment ratios signalling visible futures.

**Without it:** The Human Clock falls behind. Skills become obsolete faster than development replaces them. Trust erodes faster than communication rebuilds it. Technology sits underutilised whilst people disengage.

### 3. Modular Flexibility

Altering all three clocks (without breaking) requires adaptive capabilities: to reconfigure strategy as markets shift, adjust operations as patterns emerge, and evolve human practices as understanding deepens.

This requires an element of engineering your own luck to create structural conditions where adaptation becomes possible rather than waiting for circumstances to force change.

The theory for this proactive adaptability is precisely what Howard's research recognises: *"The organisations that thrive have built modular architectures allowing rapid reconfiguration whilst maintaining coordination. They experiment at edges without fragmenting the core."*

**Connection to SPAR:** This emerged from Chapters 6-7's convergence principles creating integration points that flex without fragmenting, and a modular architecture that enables reconfiguration without rebuilding.

**Without it:** Rigidity in any clock constrains all others. Strategic inflexibility prevents operational experimentation. Operational brittleness blocks strategic pivots. Human resistance stalls both.

## Evidence of Trinity Foundations in Practice

IMD research reveals how these foundations operate in practice.

- **L'Oréal** maintains a startup mindset despite its scale, showing *Modular Flexibility*, the ability to rapidly reconfigure teams and resources around new opportunities.
- **Coca-Cola** demonstrates *Synchronisation*, aligning data infrastructure with decision cadence across functions through democratised data access and evidence-based decision-making.
- **Mastercard** and **DBS** exemplify *Human-Centric Augmentation*, using AI to elevate analyst judgement in fraud detection rather than replace it.
- **NVIDIA's** evolution from gaming to AI infrastructure shows *Modular Flexibility* applied at enterprise scale.

There is a critical failure mode that Howard warns against: *"Many organisations eliminate data bottlenecks in one area, whilst other functions remain data-starved. They solve technical problems locally without addressing coordination systemically. This creates islands of capability that cannot coordinate when convergence demands enterprise-wide synchronisation."*

I regularly speak with companies failing to integrate and align and, worse still, not even being aware of the reasons for their difficulties. They celebrate green metrics in each domain, but the clocks are unsynchronised beneath the surface

This is why the Trinity assessment is so critical. It reveals the coordination gaps that organisational structure hides. Your score shows where boundaries prevent the synchronisation that AI demands.

## The Leadership Shift: Developing your *Conductor Capabilities*

Based on your lowest Trinity scoring, focus your leadership practice to strengthen that foundation first. The capabilities below aren't sequential, but ongoing practices that compound over time. Use this as a recovery and guide rather than a checklist.

1. **Synchronised Rhythm:** When speed outruns judgement, coordination breaks. Strategy pivots faster than teams can stabilise decisions, creating chaos rather than deliberate progress.

**Capability to strengthen:** Judgement Under Ambiguity

**Daily practice:** Distinguish when to pause and when to accelerate. For high-impact decisions where human consequences outweigh technical gains, slow down deliberately and capture why timing matters. For low-risk, reversible decisions, accelerate without waiting for perfect certainty. Use dual lenses before committing: Personal (logic, values, instinct from Chapter 3) and Enterprise (Board Consult voices from Chapter 5).

You know it's strengthening when teams can explain when to move fast or slow without escalation, and decisions feel intentional rather than pressured.

2. **Human-Centric Augmentation:** When AI capability advances faster than people's confidence or skills, coordination breaks. Productivity rises whilst trust erodes quietly until resistance surfaces.

**Capability to strengthen:** Trust Stewardship

**Daily practice:** Apply the +3/-2 anchor rule from Chapter 1. For every signal suggesting efficiency over people (automation, headcount reduction, process standardisation), create three visible investments in human futures (development, mobility, new responsibilities). Track the people-to-technology investment ratio monthly. Run Trust Checkpoints asking: Is AI strengthening human judgement or replacing it?

You know it's strengthening when people describe feeling stretched and growing, not overwhelmed or replaceable. Innovation experiments increase alongside efficiency gains.

3. **Modular Flexibility:** When work still moves through sequential handoffs despite decisions requiring simultaneous input, coordination breaks and functional excellence will prevent enterprise agility.

## Capability to strengthen: Enterprise Orchestration

**Daily practice:** Redesign one workflow from sequential approvals to parallel contribution around shared outcomes. Replace one functional metric with an enterprise value measure. Use all four Board Consult voices for cross-functional decisions, ensuring Strategy, Operations, Risk, and People perspectives inform choices before commitment.

You know it's strengthening when strategy shifts no longer trigger reorganisations. Teams reconfigure around priorities without losing coherence.

## Adaptive Learning: The Capability That Sustains All Three

Learning must compound faster than complexity grows. It's the foundation to coordinate under pressure rather than relying on improvement by trial and error.

Continuous practice: Run 15-minute learning loops after major decisions asking: What did AI recommend? What did we decide? Why did judgement override or confirm the recommendation? Establish reverse mentoring to normalise learning across hierarchy. Measure confident judgement and insight reuse, not training completion.

You know it's strengthening when lessons travel faster than problems. Teams reference previous decisions as learning and as a result, capability will compound instead of fragment.

These capabilities strengthen one another. Focus on your weakest Trinity area first, and the others improve alongside it. Without integration, each undermines the rest:

- Judgement without trust creates pace nobody follows.
- Orchestration without learning cannot adapt.
- Trust without judgement drifts into slow consensus.

The leadership shift becomes clear: authority gives way to orchestration, certainty moves to sensing, individual performance evolves to system capability.

## From Readiness To Results

Your Trinity score revealed your coordination reality. Most organisations score between 15 and 23 points (see Appendix F), indicating component readiness but coordination vulnerability. This is not failure, it's awareness that allows deliberate strengthening before deployment pressure exposes gaps. Once you diagnose where coordination breaks and which *Conductor Capabilities* require strengthening, much of the battle has already been fought.

I urge you to move away from traditional readiness assessments to the coordination practice outlined in this chapter. Focus on your weakest Trinity area first and you will soon experience rhythm starting to identify desynchronisation before it becomes a crisis.

Howard's research indicates that component excellence without coordination delivers technical success whilst creating zero enterprise value. This is simply efficient mediocrity. Those who maintain strong Trinity integration sustain coordination even when complexity grows, preserving capability under pressure and delivering converged enterprise value.

You're ready when your Three Clocks move in coherent rhythm, not when all components individually show green.

**Ritual**: Quarterly Trinity Review with cross-functional leaders: re-score all 15 questions, identify desynchronisation patterns before they become critical, address gaps whilst correction remains inexpensive (90 minutes).

**Metric:** Trinity Integration Score, percentage of 15 questions answered 'yes, with evidence' across Synchronised Rhythm, Human-Centric Augmentation, and Modular Flexibility. Target 80%+ (24+ points), tracked monthly to catch erosion early.

**If You Remember One Thing:** Readiness is not component completion but coordination capability. When your Three Clocks move in a coherent rhythm, high-quality execution can be delivered whilst under pressure. Without the coordination, even excellent components will join the 70% to 95% of programmes that fail. The work now is practical, so start building coordination deliberately through observable leadership behaviours.

**Where This Takes You Next:** Now we consider how leaders can maintain synchronised rhythms when deployment pressure mounts and functions fragment.

CHAPTER 11

# FROM READINESS TO RESULTS

# Orchestrating ownership

The promise to Lead with AI and Stay Human reaches its ultimate test in implementation. This is where theory meets execution pressure, and transformation meets reality. Failure at this stage rarely stems from weak vision, limited capability, or inadequate technology. The real breakdown occurs when readiness meets reality, and when AI acceleration exposes coordination gaps no traditional hierarchy was designed to handle.

We have reached the point in the journey where leadership is no longer about insight, strategy, or capability; it's about maintaining coordination discipline when execution pressure mounts and functions fragment.

Resistance is rarely refusal; it shows up as coordination friction under pressure. Even with strong leadership alignment, clear strategy, and modern systems, execution slows or fractures when coordination mechanisms fail to evolve at the same pace as AI acceleration. AI compresses time, increases interdependence, and removes the luxury of sequential decision-making. Yet most organisations still operate as if work moves in stages.

Traditional hierarchies rely on these sequential workflows; one team completes its task, hands over, and starts again. Many organisations function like a relay race, efficient only if each baton pass is perfectly timed. AI transforms this dynamic. Work now resembles synchronised swimming, where every function moves at once — distinct, yet interdependent — each motion affecting the rhythm of the whole.

Legacy organisational design worked with fixed lanes and handoffs, whereas AI forces simultaneous motion. AI doesn't just speed up the swimmers, it introduces algorithmic currents that no single function can see alone. Without orchestration, each team optimises only for its own strokes rather than the routine.

This mismatch between continuous workflows and stop-start structures is why many transformations stall. When pressure mounts, teams retreat to familiar patterns: escalation meetings, alignment decks, and decision-by-committee — all in an attempt to restore control at the cost of flow.

Performance wiring compounds the problem. Behaviour will always follow reward, and when KPIs remain functionally anchored, coordination becomes optional rather than essential. True enterprise performance demands metrics that reinforce shared value, not isolated optimisation. The most successful organisations I've worked with changed their measures first, aligning performance indicators to enterprise value before expecting cross-functional rhythm to hold.

This is where readiness and results diverge. Readiness gives you the capacity to act; coordination, when supported by coherent performance systems, turns that capacity into movement.

If you scored 14 or above in the Trinity assessment, you've already confirmed the foundations are strong: synchronised clocks, human-centric augmentation, and modular flexibility. What you need now are coordination muscles that hold those rhythms steady under real execution pressure.

To help this process, we will examine two organisations that have crossed this threshold. Bayer's Dynamic Shared Ownership demonstrates how trust, rights, and language make coordination operational. DBS Bank demonstrates how disciplined orchestration becomes a competitive advantage.

Together, they illustrate the shift from preparation to performance. Coordination can no longer rely on goodwill, escalation, or alignment rituals, but requires operating discipline.

## Two Organisations Demonstrating the Right Discipline

### Case Study 1:

**Bayer's Dynamic Shared Ownership:** Trust as Coordination Foundation

Bayer's effort to flatten a twelve-layer hierarchy into Dynamic Shared Ownership (DSO) is one of the most ambitious organisational reshapes in recent corporate history. Since 2023, DSO has sought to build trust in a new system and in one another by empowering individuals to make faster and better decisions closer to where work happens. The principle is that when ownership is shared, coordination becomes distributed rather than delegated. The challenge, however, is ensuring that shared ownership becomes operational, not merely aspirational.

Early pilots produced measurable gains. In Southeast Asia, launch dates advanced by five to nine months, processes were shortened by 60%, and €2 million in new value was generated within sixty days. These results came not from structural change alone, but from systematic operational shifts that made shared ownership work daily.

## Structural Foundation

Bayer eliminated approval layers for decisions below defined thresholds, giving local market teams direct authority for customer-facing choices without regional sign-off. A decision-rights matrix clarified where independent action was permitted and where coordination was required. CEO Bill Anderson slashed Bayer's 1,362-page rule book by 99%, not to reduce protection, but to create clarity about what decisions needed coordination versus what required speed.

Decision cycles shortened from yearly reviews to 90-day rhythms, accelerating the speed at which teams could act without losing alignment.

## Process Reshape

Standing meetings dropped by 40%, replaced with asynchronous updates. Bayer introduced 48-hour decision sprints for cross-functional choices that had previously taken weeks. Clear escalation rules determined when issues required broader input. Collaboration spaces replaced email chains, making decision rationale visible and reusable. Coordination became embedded in flow, freeing time for execution whilst preserving alignment.

## Incentive Alignment

Performance shifted from functional metrics to cross-functional outcomes. Individual advancement depended on collective success. When career progression required enabling others, coordination became a necessity, not a courtesy.

## Cultural Enabler

Language reinforced these shifts. Traditional coordination language such as *escalate* and *seek approval* was replaced with flow-oriented verbs such as *apply protocol*, *submit input*, and *resolve tension*. This linguistic discipline signalled intent and created psychological safety.

Diana Scholz, Global Communications Leader for Bayer's Consumer Health division, observes this cultural shift. *"Words always matter. When leaders use aligned language, it creates safety and trust. Resources become decision-makers. Managing people becomes enabling teams. The early pilots proved that when trust and coordination rise together, speed follows naturally. But the real challenge is sustaining that trust when the system is under pressure."*

## Case Study 2:

**DBS Bank:** Turning Discipline into Competitive Advantage

DBS Bank, headquartered in Singapore, has transformed itself from 'dinosaur' to 'world's best bank'. Within less than a decade, it became a global benchmark for digital leadership, not because of technology, but through disciplined coordination.

DBS replaced functional silos with cross-functional customer-journey teams, accountable for end-to-end outcomes through what they call journey governance.

Tan Su Shan, the CEO of DBS, is reported to have said, "*We are organised by customer journeys so there is clear end-to-end ownership and understanding of who is accountable, and how they can empower the team.*"

Additionally, their planning cadences are synchronised across functions, and they design with a joint focus on both customer and employee experience.

Journey governance embedded Trinity-style readiness into daily operations: context was shared, rights were made clear, and the rhythm was consistent. Dependencies across technology, operations, risk, and channels were identified before execution, not after delays occurred.

Journey owners had the authority to resolve cross-functional trade-offs within set timeframes. When conflicts emerged, escalation was predefined. Decisions travelled horizontally, not vertically.

Results were substantial: faster time-to-market, lower costs, greater agility, and repeated recognition as the *World's Best Bank*.

DBS proved that readiness creates the capability to act, but systematic coordination turns capability into results. This marks the shift from preparation to performance.

## The Coordination System: CROS in Practice

Both Bayer and DBS demonstrate systematic approaches and coordination discipline. I developed CROS to replicate this, and its four elements form a progressive discipline:

| Context | Rights | Orchestration | Synthesis |
|---|---|---|---|
| **Map dependencies** before they paralyse. | **Define who leads** before conflict emerges. | **Coordinate input** without meeting overload. | **Create decisions** so they travel. |
| Surface cross-functional ripple effects early so strategy can move without being stalled by hidden dependencies. | Distributed decision-making works only when authority boundaries are explicit and escalation paths clear. | Replace recurring alignment meetings with structured asynchronous input to expose real trade-offs fast. | Produce portable, explicit decisions that cascade cleanly across functions and build reusable trade-offs fast. |
| • Reveal interdependencies before work begins.<br>• Translate strategic intent into operational clartity. | • Proximity rights: closest function leads.<br>• Adjacent functions validate within fixed windows. | • Gather structured async input.<br>• Shift collaboration from debate to integration. | • One-page decision summaries.<br>• Make trade-offs explicit and portable. |

*CROS turns strategic intent into coordinated execution at AI speed – a leadership discipline that strengthens with practice.*

Traditional project management tools like RACI charts, steering committees, and stakeholder analyses were designed for sequential handoffs. They cannot handle AI's simultaneous, cross-functional workflows. CROS addresses this gap.

CROS isn't a strict process, but a muscle to strengthen. It builds capability through repetition in the flow of work. Over time, coordination at AI speed becomes reflex rather than effort. *(For detailed CROS templates, examples, and 90-day implementation plan, see Appendix D)*

### **Context:** Mapping Dependencies Before They Paralyse

Under AI acceleration, coordination fails when dependencies are discovered too late. Stakeholder analysis asks who needs information. Context mapping asks how decisions ripple across boundaries and prevents paralysis before it starts. Without clearly translating context, big ideas can't be realised. Clarity might exist, but coordination capability is never initiated.

DBS Bank institutionalised this through *journey governance*, i.e., planning and reviewing by customer journeys rather than by functions. Journey mapping surfaced multi-departmental dependencies before they became bottlenecks. This is context translation at scale, turning strategic clarity into actionable guidance that each function can implement.

Tan Su Shan has said, "*My advice to leaders is to be focused and practical. You need to pick your spots, align your teams, and empower them to execute. At DBS, we use a simple lens called 'PURE', Products, Usage, Risk, and Economics — to keep teams grounded while moving fast.*" When Context translation works, synchronised clocks stay aligned. Speed is then possible because people, data, and decision rhythms are coordinated.

Bayer's experience illustrated this principle. Before a critical global conference, Diana discovered that assumed alignment wasn't coordination in practice. "*We assumed alignment and shared ownership of outcomes were handled because everyone knew about the initiative. What we discovered was that knowing about a horizontal project doesn't mean understanding how it intersects with your function's authority or what coordination is required.*"

Even when context is translated with the best of intentions, gaps will still arise. In this case, the issue was identified early enough to rebuild clarity and restore coordination before the conference took place, but remember, this is a continual process.

Context mapping is the **first act of orchestration** and the foundation that connects strategic intent with daily execution and prevents readiness from unravelling into confusion.

### **Rights:** Establishing Authority Before Conflicts Emerge

Under execution pressure, distributed decision power collapses when authority boundaries are unclear. In decentralised organisations, decision-making only works when authority boundaries are explicit. Without predefined rights, functions will collide because each require different needs and goals. Who prevails?

My answer is proximity rights: The function closest to the decision context leads, and adjacent functions validate feasibility within defined timeframes. As an example, demand-related calls should sit with Sales or Marketing and be validated by Operations. If capacity fails, escalation follows a defined path rather than descending into endless debate.

DBS Bank's Managing through Journeys (MtJs) enables it to function as a Horizontal Organisation, with cross-functional teams collaborating. Each journey owner has the authority to resolve trade-offs within fixed time frames with clear escalation protocols when boundaries are exceeded. Clarity of rights enables speed without hierarchy and prevents paralysis under pressure. The annual report links this change to improved customer satisfaction in consumer and SME banking.

When informed by human-centric augmentation, these rights systems do more than define authority; they preserve expertise at the decision point whilst letting AI manage coordination overhead. This balance turns distributed decision-making from chaos into competitive advantage.

#### **Orchestration:** Coordination Without Meeting Overhead

When coordination lacks structure, AI acceleration produces meetings instead of movement. Operational orchestration achieves the opposite. Collaboration happens efficiently through structured, asynchronous input, followed by a focused synthesis session. Each function submits its assumptions, constraints, and recommendations in advance. The synthesis conversation then centres not on 'who's right' but on how diverse inputs integrate to make the system smarter.

At DBS, journey teams used templates to collect structured input showing real trade-offs. The result was fewer meetings and higher decision quality.

As Diana observed at Bayer, replacing repetitive alignment meetings with structured input revealed just a handful of true dependencies. The focus shifted from debate to design, turning collaboration into flow, not friction.

### **Synthesis:** Decisions That Travel Across Functions

Coordination breaks when decisions don't travel. Inputs matter only if they lead to choices that are clear enough to be executed consistently across functions. At Bayer, teams use 'decision one-pagers' to record both *what* was decided and *why*, in language every function understands. DBS applies the same discipline through journey scorecards shared across product, tech, and operations.

As coordination accelerates, the learning rate introduced in Chapter 8 increases as well; every solved challenge becomes reusable knowledge. CROS thus doubles as a learning architecture that prevents organisational amnesia and builds the judgement capital competitors can't replicate.

## From Individual Excellence to Enterprise Orchestration

"*Challenging myself, I had to decide what I must release,*" Diana explains. "*My mindset had to evolve, to coach more, release control and execution pride, and help others create greater combined value.*"

This orchestration discipline does not come naturally. Under pressure, even experienced leaders default to stepping in, becoming the integration point rather than building the coordination system itself.

Because orchestration has not previously been demanded of leaders, it must be learned deliberately. That requires time, practice, and the willingness to develop new skills that build capability not only in ourselves, but in others.

Diana's evolution from communications management to what she calls '*alignment orchestration*' shows what this shift looks like in practice. Her success metrics moved from personal output to system capability.

Today, she architects workflows that balance human expertise and AI capability across boundaries — not directing performance, but enabling coordinated progress.

This shift is no longer optional for leaders. CROS provides the structure, but it is leadership discipline that makes coordination operational. Orchestration becomes the art of maintaining rhythm rather than controlling outcomes.

That discipline only holds when the foundations are in place. Trust, clarity, and modular flexibility turn letting go of career-limiting recklessness into a calculated leadership risk. Without these foundations, CROS degrades into process documentation that looks aligned but fails under pressure.

This is what conventional leadership models rarely teach: coordination is not achieved by retaining authority, but by designing conditions where others can exercise it responsibly. Orchestration is the shift from directing performance to enabling coordinated progress. This is the shift from individual excellence to enterprise orchestration. This is leadership courage. It's the choice to orchestrate network capability rather than optimise individual excellence, and it's what differentiates Conductors from performers. They are leaders who amplify the collective.

## Building Your Coordination System

I recommend you start small and chose one AI-driven decision involving multiple functions. Apply CROS to that single coordination challenge, then expand as capability develops. Within ninety days you will see coordination time start to drop, trust will rise, and decisions requiring rework will decrease.

## Integration with SPAR and Forward Momentum

The coordination discipline described here unites all four SPAR capabilities:

**Strengthen** built the trust foundation for cross-boundary decisions through visible accountability and clear identity.

**Partner** created a structured challenge to overcome functional bias through AI sparring and integrative thinking.

**Amplify** developed *Conductor Capability* across silos through convergence structures, continuous learning, and trust-preserving transformation.

**Reshape** now applies these through CROS to enable horizontal workflows within vertical organisations.

Solid coordination amplifies judgement when it removes confusion and gives leaders the structure to apply discernment to create value. When Diana helped establish customer-proximity decision rights at Bayer, and when DBS empowered journey owners with clear authority, neither restricted power; they removed the friction that hindered decisions altogether.

CROS provides the structure for faster, better cross-functional decisions, because everyone understands both their authority and their limits.

But CROS can only operate on solid foundations. Without synchronised clocks, Context translation fails as functions move at different speeds. Without human-centric augmentation, Rights protocols optimise efficiency but erode expertise. Without modular readiness, Orchestration relies on heroics rather than coordinated capability built on trust.

When these conditions are in place, CROS scales and sustains coordination. It becomes the operating rhythm for AI-era leadership, where readiness turns into results and judgement flows through the system as confidently as data itself.

**If You Remember One Thing:** AI transformations fail not because organisations aren't ready, but because coordination can't keep pace with cross-functional dependencies. CROS was introduced as the discipline that turns readiness into results, ensuring that human judgement flows cleanly across the enterprise.

**Where This Takes You Next:** We have now seen two examples of organisations that demonstrate the discipline to apply everything this book is advocating: leadership that stays human whilst evolving to move at

AI speed. Coordination cannot rely on heroic personal effort. It relies on a system where judgement can flow: Context keeps clocks synchronised, Rights clarity preserves expertise, Orchestration is structured without suffocating, and Synthesis ensures learning compounds.

My promise of *Lead with AI. Stay Human.* is not that AI makes work easier. It is that when you Strengthen identity, Partner with intelligence, Amplify capability, and Reshape for flow, you build organisations where humans and AI elevate each other and no longer compete.

The window for developing this capability is closing — not because AI will replace you, but because leaders who orchestrate at AI speed are already executing whilst others are still watching.

Your readiness is assessed.

Your coordination discipline is defined.

What remains is the choice to lead differently than you were previously taught.

CONCLUSION

# ELEVATE POTENTIAL

# *The leader's new compass*

When I finally stopped running and started listening, I realised that what needed to change was not just how I worked, but why. I had spent years optimising for speed, delivery, and control, inside a firm that claimed people were the greatest asset whilst rewarding extraction over development.

My purpose has always been clear, but I needed realignment. Through conversations with leaders across the world — different industries and contexts — I again matched my values with my voice and actions.

That belief is rooted in a simple truth: that investment in people compounds over time, and that AI becomes a force that grows potential rather than replaces it. As these conversations unfolded, the same questions surfaced again and again:

- How do we move faster without losing judgement?
- How do we scale trust when algorithms accelerate decisions?
- How do we elevate people when pressure rewards extraction?

Through SPAR, you have built the capability to strengthen your identity, partner with intelligence, amplify coordination, and reshape for flow. The Four Voices ensure decisions reflect enterprise reality. The Three Clocks help orchestrate different speeds. CROS provides the discipline to maintain coordination under pressure. Together, these form a leadership operating system for staying human whilst moving at AI speed.

AI is democratising expertise. Knowledge that once defined authority is now instantly accessible. This creates an uncomfortable question for leaders: *If AI can do my work, what is my value?*

The answer is not less expertise, but elevated expertise:

- Experts define guardrails, not approvals.
- Leaders orchestrate intelligence, not answers.
- Teams compound capability, not just output.
- Value emerges from coordination, not optimisation.

This is the leadership inflection point. Leadership is moving from owning expertise to orchestrating enterprise value — and from extracting performance to elevating potential.

That is how modern leaders orchestrate enterprise value: by allowing judgement to travel through the system at speed, guided by trust, learning, and clear coordination.

The question is whether you will build that capability deliberately — or wait until pressure forces it.

## The Choice Ahead

You now stand at a crossroads.

One path continues to reward speed, extraction, and local optimisation, but risks fracture. The other invests deliberately in coordination, trust, and learning, enabling organisations to move faster without breaking apart.

This is not my own idealism. It is practical leadership for an AI-accelerated world that still values humanity. The organisations that thrive will not be those that automate most aggressively, but those that elevate most deliberately.

Start small. Start now.

This week, choose one decision you are facing and, before acting (see Appendix E):

- Engage all Four Voices — not just the one that feels urgent
- Check whether your Clocks are synchronised
- Ask whether this choice elevates potential or extracts performance
- Make the trade-offs visible to your team

Then help one other leader do the same.

Leadership is not a position. It is a pattern. When enough leaders change the pattern, the system changes with them.

AI will continue to accelerate. The Strategic Clock will tick faster. Operations will demand more speed. But the Human Clock — where meaning, trust, and judgement take root — still needs time.

Our role as leaders is not to force all clocks to match AI's pace, but to conduct their different rhythms into something greater: organisations that move at the speed of technology whilst retaining the wisdom of humanity.

Speed and cost optimisation are short-lived. What endures — and what creates fulfilment — is elevating potential with purpose, sustainably.

That rhythm starts with you.
One leader who chooses to Strengthen, Partner, Amplify, and Reshape.
Then another.
Then a team.
Then an enterprise.

And this is how we *Lead with AI. Stay Human.*

This is how we transform organisations from machines that extract value into systems that compound potential.

*Elevate Potential*

*The future belongs not to those who optimise for speed, but to those who elevate potential with purpose.*

## The Leader's Compass

How Modern Leaders Orchestrate Enterprise Value

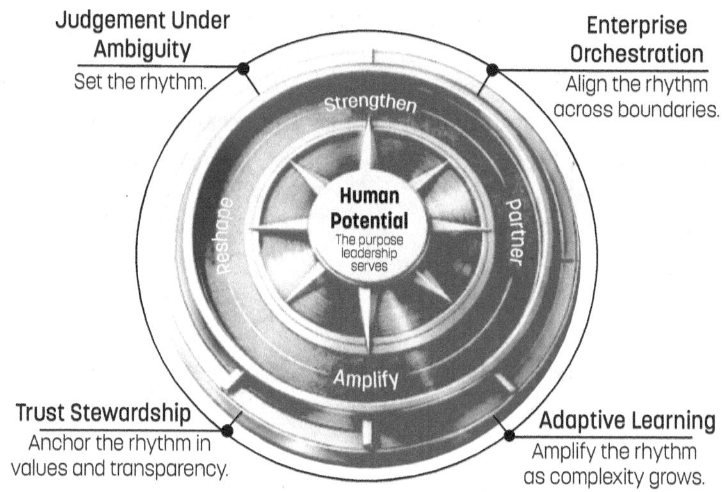


Lead with clarity. Elevate with purpose.

PeterWhealy.com

# GRATITUDE

*This book would not have been possible without the many good (and even bad) leaders with whom I've had the privilege of working during my career. Also, the people who have inspired and helped me and also patiently listened to my many ramblings. I'm also deeply grateful to each of the following individuals for their insight and inspiration that contributed to this book and made it a rich and fulfilling learning experience for its readers:*

- **Mark Abraham:** Global Head Org Design @ Rightmove
- **Sally-Anne Airey:** CEO @ Skilful Leaders
- **Caroline Barth:** CHRO @ Syngenta Group
- **Ulrik Brix:** CEO @ NOCA
- **Marcio Brochado Correia:** CDI Officer @ dsm-firmenich Animal Nutrition & Health
- **Simon Brown:** CLO @ Big Four Consultancy
- **Antonio Calco' Labruzzo:** Senior Vice President People and Culture @ Arcera Life Sciences
- **Karolina Cardoso:** Global Head of Reward @ Givaudan
- **Michiel van Duin:** Chief People Technology, Data and Insights Officer @ Novartis
- **Pablo Ettinger:** Founding Member @ Caffè Nero
- **Pete Jaworski:** Head of People Data & Analytics @ Maersk
- **Charles Jennings:** Co-founder @ 70:20:10 institute
- **Miriam Kugel:** AI Transformation @ Microsoft

- **Keith O'Loughlin:** CEO @ Everlough Holdings
- **Massimo Muzzi:** VP Strategy & Sustainability @ ABB Electrification
- **Hemerson Paes:** Senior Global Network Catalyst @ Roche
- **Andrea Petrone:** CEO @ Andrea Petrone
- **Diana Scholz:** Head of Global Communications @ Bayer Consumer Health
- **Antony Shields:** Global People Operations Director @ Baker McKenzie
- **Amit A. Sidhpura:** Global Business Strategy @ IBM and Founder of CityMonk
- **Rebecca Snow**: Global People & Organisation VP @ Mars Incorporated
- **Alessandro Ventura:** Global VP Technology & Transformation @ Unilever
- **Angelique de Vries:** President EMEA @ Workday
- **Ernst Wühr:** CEO @ EMS
- **Amy Edmondson** @ Harvard Business School
- **Rita McGrath** @ Columbia Business School
- **Howard Yu** @ IMD Business School

# ABOUT THE AUTHOR

Peter Whealy is a leadership strategist and founder of Elevate Potential, a consultancy specialising in AI-enabled leadership transformation. A former Big Four Equity Partner who led Learning and Leadership across Switzerland, he spent 30 years helping Fortune 500 organisations navigate transformation. In his work, he advises global organisations and boards, writes on emerging people and leadership topics, and delivers keynotes on a broad range of people-related topics. He lives in the French Alps with his much-loved four boys and dog (Jay), where he can pursue his love of nature and adventure sports.

## Continue the Conversation

Share your implementation stories and what you learned with your team. Join the community of practice at:

*PeterWhealy.com*

APPENDIX

# LEADERSHIP PRACTICE TOOLKIT

This appendix is a *working toolkit* where each page stands alone and can be reused with teams, peers, or boards.

# APPENDIX A:
## SPAR FRAMEWORK AT A GLANCE

SPAR is a leadership rhythm, not a one-off intervention. It describes how leaders evolve themselves and their organisations in the AI era.

### Strengthen

**Focus:** Leadership identity and judgement

- Reconnect purpose before accelerating action.
- Use AI as a sparring partner, not an oracle.
- Integrate logic, values, and instinct.

**Shifts from:** Individual execution → Quality of judgement

### Partner

**Focus:** Trust and disciplined collaboration

- Make assumptions and trade-offs explicit.
- Design decisions that travel with context.
- Build trust through transparency under pressure.

**Shifts from:** Functional optimisation → Enterprise coherence

## Amplify

**Focus:** Capability at scale

- Embed learning into the flow of work.
- Replace training events with developmental work design.
- Ensure learning rate exceeds change velocity.

**Shifts from:** Knowledge accumulation → Capability compounding

## Reshape

**Focus:** Systems and incentives

- Reshape structures around outcomes, not functions.
- Align metrics to enterprise value creation.
- Celebrate elevation, not extraction.

**Shifts from:** Control systems → Enabling systems

# APPENDIX B:

## THE FOUR *CONDUCTOR CAPABILITIES*

These capabilities describe *how leadership works* when expertise is distributed and speed unavoidable.

### 1. Judgement Under Ambiguity

**Purpose:** Set strategic tempo.

- Know when to pause for reflection.
- Know when to accelerate for learning.

**Replaces:** waiting for certainty
**Enables:** confident action without false clarity

### 2. Enterprise Orchestration

**Purpose:** Make decisions travel.

- Align context across boundaries.
- Preserve coherence under pressure.

**Replaces:** coordination meetings
**Enables:** flow across functions

### 3. Trust Stewardship

**Purpose:** Anchor speed to values.

- Make trade-offs visible.
- Act consistently under pressure.

**Replaces:** trust as sentiment
**Enables:** trust as operational discipline

### 4. Adaptive Learning

**Purpose:** Compound capability

- Capture learning from real work.
- Retire failed patterns quickly.

**Replaces:** periodic training
**Enables:** continuous organisational intelligence

# APPENDIX C:
## THE AI BOARD CONSULT (FOUR VOICES)

*A discipline for strengthening decisions before they scale.*

Most AI-driven decisions fail not because of poor analysis, but because critical perspectives were never invited into the room. The AI Board Consult is not a governance forum or approval step. It is a thinking discipline designed to expose blind spots early, when they are still cheap to fix.

Before committing to any significant AI-enabled decision, deliberately test it through the Four Voices.

### 1. Future Impact

**Question:** *In three years, what needs to be true for this to be considered a success?*

This voice pulls the decision out of short-term optimisation and into strategic consequence.

It asks:

- What capabilities must exist for this to work sustainably?
- What dependencies does this create we'll have to live with later?
- What future constraints are we locking in today?

**What it prevents:** short-term wins that create long-term fragility

## 2. Risk & Ethics

**Question:** *What could go catastrophically wrong?*

This is not about compliance theatre or pessimism. It is about **surfacing irreversible downside** before speed makes it invisible.

It asks:

- Where could this decision fail silently?
- What risks scale faster than our ability to respond?
- What would be hardest to undo once deployed?

**What it prevents:** reputational damage, ethical drift, and compound risk

## 3. People Proxy

**Question:** *Who is affected, and how will they actually experience this?*

This voice represents those **not in the decision room** but most impacted by the outcome.

It asks:

- Who gains clarity, and who loses agency?
- What uncertainty does this create for people?
- Does this expand or narrow future opportunity?

**What it prevents:** resistance, disengagement, and trust erosion disguised as efficiency

## 4. Implementation Realist

**Question:** *What will actually break during execution?*

This voice grounds ambition in operational reality.

It asks:

- Where will coordination fail first?
- What assumptions rely on perfect handoffs?
- What will teams work around rather than escalate?

**What it prevents:** elegant strategies that collapse on contact with reality

Using the Four Voices: either solo (10 minutes of structured thinking), in pairs (sparring partner dynamic), or scaled to your team (distributed perspective gathering).

## How to Apply

- Apply it before scale, not after problems emerge.
- Use AI to *generate challenge*, not to close debate.
- Capture key insights in one page so decisions travel with context.
- Treat overrides and tensions as learning, not friction.

The goal is not consensus but decision resilience, choices that hold when pressure rises.

# APPENDIX D:

## CROS TO COORDINATE AT SPEED

CROS is the coordination muscle that turns readiness into results. Use the following 90-day plan to assist you. You should see reduced coordination time, higher trust across functions, and fewer decisions requiring rework or escalation.

| Phase | Focus | Key Output |
|---|---|---|
| Days 1–7 | Diagnostic | A context map of one stalled AI-driven decision, identifying conflicting data, rights, and dependencies |
| Days 8–21 | Rights & Orchestration | Clear decision rights and a lightweight orchestration process replacing unstructured meetings |
| Days 22–30 | Synthesis | A one-page decision artefact that travels across functions with clear ownership |
| Months 2–3 | Capability Build | Two or more decisions coordinated using CROS; a second trained 'Conductor'; a shared decision library |

The coordination capability built through CROS becomes the foundation for sustained transformation. Your role is to keep the orchestration consistent through changing conditions and competitive pressure.

# APPENDIX E:
## YOUR MONDAY DECISION

Use this reflection for one real decision this week.

Before deciding, ask:

1. Am I deciding from purpose or pressure?
2. What assumption am I accepting without challenge?
3. What trade-offs am I making — and are they visible?
4. Who else should validate this before it locks?
5. What would I do differently if speed were not rewarded?

Then act.

Write one sentence: What human judgement did I apply that AI could not?

Repeat weekly. Teach others.

*These practices are not theory. They are the operating discipline of leaders who elevate potential in the AI era.*

# APPENDIX F:

## TRINITY READINESS SCAN

### Interpreting Your Trinity Score

| Score | Zone | What It Means | Your Action |
|---|---|---|---|
| **24-30 points** | **Green: Deploy with Confidence** | Strong Trinity integration. Coordination capability exists systematically, not just in exceptional teams. Component readiness AND coordination capability are both present. | Proceed with scaled deployment whilst maintaining Trinity vigilance. Establish quarterly Trinity reviews (90 minutes with cross-functional leaders). Monitor score monthly, targeting 24+ maintenance. Document what enabled integration so that capability transfers to new initiatives. Share coordination mechanisms with other business units preparing for deployment. |
| **15-23 points** | **Yellow: Strengthen Before Scaling** | Mixed integration. Some capabilities strong, others weak. Component readiness likely high but coordination capability inconsistent. This is the most common zone and most addressable if acknowledged honestly. Technical capability exists, but integration gaps will emerge catastrophically under deployment pressure. | Identify your weakest capability (subtotal scored 0-6 out of 10). See 'Building *Conductor Capabilities*' section for specific behaviours to practice strengthening that capability this week. Run limited pilots specifically testing coordination under pressure. Reassess in 60-90 days. Don't proceed to full scale until reaching Green (24+ score). |
| **0-14 points** | **Red: Return to Foundation-Building** | Weak Trinity integration across the foundations. Component completion may look impressive, but coordination capability is largely absent. The gap between component readiness and coordination capability is catastrophic. Proceeding from this zone joins the high statistical failure rate. | Stop deployment planning. Return to systematic capability building: SPAR development (Chapters 1-8) builds integrated personal and team capability. Chapter 9 establishes a trust foundation and *Conductor Capabilities* as an integrated system (not isolated skills). Address Trinity gaps through 6-12- month systematic development, not quick fixes. Reassess quarterly until reaching Yellow. Minimum six months before proceeding. Better to delay deliberately than fail publicly. |

# AI USAGE DISCLOSURE

In keeping with this book's central message, I partnered with frontier AI models to elevate my own potential, using them to stress-test assumptions, surface counterarguments, and accelerate synthesis. The outputs were grounded in my writing, ideas, extensive practitioner experience, and from interviews with senior leaders who shared their real-world implementation insights. Every decision, edit, and judgement was mine. All content was reviewed, edited, and fact-checked against source material. No proprietary data was exposed to AI systems. The voice, choices, and accountability are entirely mine, and I take full responsibility for the final text.

www.ingramcontent.com/pod-product-compliance
Lightning Source LLC
LaVergne TN
LVHW050955080826
845145LV00006B/1510
* 9 7 8 1 9 1 8 2 1 5 1 5 1 *